WORK MATTERS

COMPLETE
LETTER
WRITER

TIM & JENNY SAVILLE

WARD LOCK

© Ward Lock Limited 1961 and Revised material 1977

This edition first published in Great Britain in 1978
by Ward Lock Limited, Villiers House,
41–47 Strand, London WC2N 5JE, a Cassell company.

Reprinted 1982, 1987, 1989, 1990, 1991, 1993

Text set in Baskerville
by Cox and Wyman Ltd

Printed and bound in Great Britain

British Library Cataloguing in Publication Data
Saville, Tim
The complete letter writer. – [Revised ed.]
1. Letter writing
I. Title   II. Saville, Jenny   III. Complete
letter writing for ladies and gentlemen
808.6   PE1483

ISBN 0-7063-1066-7

Contents

Foreword 12

Introduction 13

Writing materials 13

Setting out a letter 14

Writing a personal letter 15

The love letter 16

Letters to editors 16

Letters to young children 16

Letter writing in business 16

Setting out a business letter 18

Forms of address for the commencement and conclusion of letters 21

Model letters

Formal invitations 34

Formal wedding invitation, sent by parents of bride
**Wedding invitation where the bride's parents are
  not the hosts**
Wedding invitation sent by step-parents
Acceptance of formal wedding invitation
Declining invitation to wedding
Recalling wedding invitation
Postponement of wedding invitation
**Cancellation of wedding invitation because of family
  mourning**
Formal invitation to dinner
Invitation using a printed 'At Home' card
**Formal invitations to dances, bridge parties, garden
  parties, etc.**

Announcements 38

Engagement
Forthcoming marriage
Marriage
Death
In memoriam
Wedding anniversary (Silver, Golden wedding, etc.)
Birth
Adoption
Thanks for sympathy

4

Engagement and Marriage 41

Letter to friend announcing forthcoming marriage
  or engagement (1)
(2)
Letter to a prospective son-in-law
Letter to prospective daughter-in-law
Letter to prospective parents-in-law
Letter from the set of prospective in-laws to the other
Reply to above
Letter of congratulation on an engagement
Letter to a friend upon the breaking of an engagement
Informal wedding invitation (1)
(2)
Letter to a friend asking her to be a bridesmaid
Letter to a friend asking him to act as best man
Letter of thanks for wedding present
Letter of thanks after a wedding
Letter returning engagement or wedding presents

Birth and adoption 51

Letter announcing the birth of a child
Reply to above
Letter of congratulation on the birth of a child
Letter of congratulation on adoption of a child

Condolence and bereavement 53

Letter from a widow, informing her husband's
  employers of his death
Letter from a lady to a relative, informing him of her
  husband's death and requesting assistance
Letter to a relative, asking him to attend a funeral
Letter announcing a death to a friend

Letter of condolence to the widow of a former
    employee
Reply to above
Letter of condolence (more distant)
Reply to above
Letter to friend who has just been divorced
Letter to friend in financial difficulties, enclosing a
    cheque
Letter to a friend ill in hospital (1)
                                        (2)
Letter offering help to a friend in trouble

Letters of congratulations 60

Letter of congratulation upon an 18th or 21st birthday
Congratulations note, to enclose with 18th or 21st
    birthday present
Letter of congratulation to a friend upon his son's or
    daughter's success
Letter of congratulation upon a professional success
Letter of congratulation on passing an examination

Social correspondence 62

Letter inviting a friend to stay
Reply accepting above
Reply declining
Letter of thanks for a visit
Informal invitation to a supper party
Letter of thanks after a dinner party
Invitation to a children's party
Reply accepting above
Reply declining above
Thanks afterwards

Children's education 67

Letter enquiring about a school
Letter acknowledging the principal's reply
Letter entering a child for school
Letter to a headmaster about pupil's inattention at
  school
Letter to a headmaster asking that a pupil might
  take an extra subject
Letter to a headmistress, about a backward pupil
Letter to a headmaster complaining that a pupil is
  being bullied
Letter asking that a pupil may be excused lessons
Letter asking that a pupil may be excused games
Letter to the principal of a school giving notice that a
  pupil is to be taken away (1)
                                          (2)
Letter of thanks to a son or daughter's tutor

Employment 75

Letter excusing absence from work
Letter requesting leave of absence
Letter asking for promotion
Application for an increase in salary
Letter thanking employer for salary increase
Letter of resignation
Letter enquiring about possible job vacancies
Letter requesting a job application form
Job application for a specific post
Job application letter, enclosing curriculum vitae
Curriculum vitae to accompany a job application
Letter accepting a post
Letter to present employer applying for a reference
Letter to previous employer applying for a reference
Letter giving a character reference
Letter giving a favourable reference

Letter giving a qualified reference
Letter refusing a reference
Open reference
Letter agreeing to give a reference
Letter taking up a reference
Request for temporary help

Business correspondence 90

Letter changing doctor (1)
                         (2)
Letter to a new doctor
Letter to the Inland Revenue concerning a change in
    tax coding
Letter engaging solicitor
Letter changing solicitor
Letter to solicitor asking him to change will
Letter instructing solicitor to prepare power of
    attorney
Letter to solicitor, asking him to pursue a debt
Letter to solicitor, asking him to advise about a
    claim for damages against the writer
Letter to solicitor, asking him about a claim for
    damages which the writer wishes to make
Letter to a bank, opening a current account
Letter transferring money from one account to another
Letter paying in a cheque
Letter stopping payment of a cheque
Letter instructing bank to pay standing order
Letter instructing the bank to honour a signature
Letter about an overdraft
Letter asking for overdraft facilities
Letter asking for advice about investments
Letter instructing the bank to make investments
Letter asking a bank to make enquiries
Letter asking for an increase in credit limit on a
    credit card

Letter enclosing a cheque in settlement of an account
Letter enclosing a cheque in part settlement of an account
Letter to store opening an account
Letter to hotel, enquiring about facilities for a private function
Letter to caterer or hotel, booking a function
Letter to a building society, withdrawing money
Letter to insurance company, insuring an article
Letter to insurance company, regarding car insurance
Letter reporting a car accident and making an insurance claim

Your home 111

Letter to an estate agent, asking for details of properties for sale
Letter to a private advertiser about a house for sale
Letter to estate agent, making an offer for a property
Letter to owner of house or flat for sale, making an offer
Letter to solicitor about house or flat purchase
Letter to brokers, or assurance company, regarding combined life assurance and house purchase
Letter to building society, enquiring about mortgage facilities
Letter applying for a mortgage
Letter to building society, asking for terms to pay off a mortgage
Letter to a landlord, asking for time to pay rent
Letter to landlord asking for repairs to be done
Letter to landlord, asking him to cancel a lease
Letter to landlord, asking for permission to sub-let
Letter to a builder, asking for an estimate

Letters of complaint 121

Letter of complaint to dry-cleaners
Letter complaining about delay in delivering goods
Letter to merchant about unsolicited goods
Letter disputing an account
Letter of complaint to a neighbour
Reply to above
Letter to the local council
Letter to local councillor
Letter to Member of Parliament

Travel and holidays 129

Letter confirming travel arrangements
Letter enquiring about hotel accommodation
Letter concerning lost property

Your club or society, charity work 131

Letter applying for membership of a club
Letter to secretary of a club, proposing a friend as
    member
Letter accepting club membership application
Letter from the secretary of a club, informing
    applicant of his election
Letter from club secretary, informing applicant that
    he has not been elected
Letter from club secretary, asking for payment of
    subscription
A repeated request for an unpaid subscription
Letter from club secretary, asking a member to resign
Letter of resignation from a club
Letter inviting a celebrity to give a talk
Thanks afterwards
Letter requesting someone to serve on a committee
Reply to above

Letter requesting a titled lady to open a fête
Letter requesting a celebrity to present prizes
Letter requesting a donation
Letter requesting patronage of a fund-raising effort
Letter thanking a patron

Requests, with replies 146

Letter asking a friend for a letter of introduction (1), (2)
Reply agreeing
Reply, less favourable
Reply refusing
Letter of introduction (1), (2)
Thanks for a letter of introduction
Letter of thanks for kindness to a friend
Letter asking a friend for a loan
Letter granting a loan
Letter refusing a loan (1), (2)
Letter refusing a loan but offering a gift
Letter demanding repayment of a loan (1)
(2)
Letter demanding repayment of a loan and
    threatening to take legal action
Letter to a friend asking him to act as executor
Letter to a friend asking him to act as trustee

Classified advertisements 157

Advertising a fund-raising event
Advertising a club or society to attract new members
Advertising holiday accommodation
Advertising a house or flat for sale
Advertising items for sale
Advertising for domestic help
Advertising a service
Situations wanted
Tradesman commencing business

Foreword

Although letter writing may be considered a lost art and the letter has been replaced to a great extent by the telephone, there are still many occasions where a letter is called for. Sometimes you will need a written record of a conversation or transaction, sometimes you may wish to state your case clearly to another person, sometimes you may wish to write a letter because the alternative of a phone call might be embarrassing or upsetting.

Even when a written letter really seems a necessity many people mistrust their powers of composition. This book is designed to help them. It is a practical and up-to-date guide to letter writing giving a large selection of typical letters for all occasions. The letters, of course, are not designed to be copied word for word. They are intended to serve only as a guide. In a specific situation there will be small modifications which common sense will suggest that you could use to give your letter a more personal touch.

It goes without saying that all the names, addresses and letters throughout the book are completely imaginary.

Introduction

Writing materials

To make a good impression a letter should be written with thought, well set out, and the writing paper chosen with care.

The size and quality of the paper are a matter of personal choice, though very flimsy paper sometimes looks cheap, but the paper should be unlined and should match the envelopes you are using. It is safest to use white or a pale tinted paper, avoiding very bright colours and dark blue or black ink are probably the most usual. Never use green or red ink. A ball-point pen is acceptable, but a pencil should never be used.

A typewriter is normally used for all business correspondence, and a copy taken. Personal letters are usually written by hand, though it is increasingly acceptable to type them, especially if the writer's handwriting is difficult to read.

If you are writing a letter by hand and your writing begins to wander up and down the page place a sheet of paper ruled with very thick black lines under the paper on which you are writing. The lines will show through and help you keep your writing straight.

Choose the envelope size to match your writing paper. For a social letter, most people choose the square shaped envelope rather than the longer one normally used for business correspondence. An envelope must be thick enough, so that your writing will not show through. For overseas correspondence use lightweight air mail paper and envelopes.

Envelopes should be 'Post Office Preferred.' Write the entire address carefully and clearly on the lower half of the envelope only so that it will not be obliterated by the postmark. The stamp, of course, should be put in the top right-hand corner. It is often a good idea to write your name and address at the back of the envelope, in case the letter cannot be delivered for some reason.

When you are writing to a person who may have moved away, it is a good idea to write 'Please Forward' on the envelope; as an added precaution you can write 'If undelivered, please return to' with your address on the back of the envelope.

Setting out a letter

Here are some examples of the different ways to set out a letter. It is usual to put the address of the writer in the top right-hand corner of the page, although if printed or embossed writing paper is used the address and telephone number can be placed at the top centre of the page, or printed in a line across the top of the page.

3 Barlow House,
Wright Street,
Chingford,
London E4K 77P.
Tel:

3 Barlow House,
Wright Street,
Chingford,
London E4K 77P.
Tel:

3 Barlow House,
Wright Street,
Chingford,
London
E4K 77P.
Tel:

3 Barlow House, Wright Street, Chingford, London E4K 77P.
Tel:

The date should always be written out in full, normally in the top left-hand corner of the page, below the address. There are many ways of writing the date.

Examples are: April 20, 19—
20 April 19—
20th April 19—
April 20th 19—

If you are writing a formal or commercial letter you should put the name and address of the person or organization to whom you are writing on the left-hand side of the letter. Of course you will not need to do this when writing to friends or relatives.

The first line of each paragraph is often indented and a line is often left between each paragraph.

The most common ways of finishing a letter are 'Yours faithfully', used with 'Dear Sir', 'Dear Sirs', 'Dear Madam', and 'Yours sincerely' used with 'Dear Mr Smith', 'Dear Mrs Smith', 'Dear Ms Smith' or 'Dear Miss Smith' and with 'Dear John' and 'Dear Sally'.

For the more intimate personal letters there are a number of ways of finishing the letter such as:

Yours affectionately
Your affectionate
Yours ever
Very sincerely yours
With love.

Writing a personal letter

Writing a letter is regarded by some people not as a pleasure but as a task. However these same people love to receive a letter. The only way to ensure that you will often receive interesting and enjoyable letters is to write some yourself.

How can you write a good letter? First of all make your letter personal to the man or woman you are writing to, ask after them and their family and comment on things which have interested you in their letter when you reply to it.

Write about yourself. What have you been doing? Where have you been? Even the most mundane events can be made to sound enjoyable if you write spontaneously and imagine yourself talking to your friend. If you write of a film you have seen or a book you have read, or even of the weather, write about how it affected you.

Try not to leave too long a time before answering a letter. That way the correspondence will remain fresh and interesting.

The love letter

As with any other letter do not write anything unless you mean it. Remember that it is preferable to receive a sincere but simply written letter than a flowery one full of fine phrases which the sender has copied out of a book. Do not forget that something written in a moment of passion might look very different in the cold light of day and that a quarrel by letter is virtually impossible to patch up.

Letters to editors

When writing letters to the editor of a newspaper or magazine, the golden rule is to be brief. Make the letter pithy, witty too, if the occasion demands. Letters which are likely to spark off a lively correspondence stand a good chance of publication. It goes without saying that those which contain libellous, obscene or blasphemous statements will certainly not be published by the journal in question.

Letters to young children

Letters to the young should be written in simple, lively language. Young boys are addressed on the envelope as 'Master James Smith', girls as 'Miss'.

Letter writing in business

There is nothing magic about business letters. They do not have to be couched in a mass of jargon and mumbo-jumbo. They fulfil the same functions as other types of letters and, like these, should be written in everyday language and express the writer's thoughts clearly and, if possible, briefly. Technical terms should be used only where they will clarify your meaning.

Every letter which you send is an ambassador for you and will create in the mind of the person receiving it a mental picture of you and your firm. He may get the impression that yours is an old-fashioned organization and that you are muddle-headed and pompous or he may sense that you and your company are efficient, trustworthy, friendly and anxious to help in every way.

The business letter has two main objectives : it provides a written record of the various stages of a transaction and it enables them to be carried out without personal contact.

All letters are 'selling' letters. They are selling the idea that the writer of the letter is an efficient and pleasant person with whom to do business. They are creating goodwill for the company and the writer. Whatever you are selling – an article, a service, an idea or yourself – you should follow some simple rules :

1 *Before starting a letter think out what you are going to say and how you are going to say it.*
2 *Write in simple, clear language, avoiding jargon and clichés.*
3 *Use short words in common use wherever possible. Use short sentences and short paragraphs.*
4 *Be natural, do not be afraid of letting your personality show in your correspondence. Be friendly and polite and use a little humour now and again when you feel that the letter warrants it.*
5 *Be direct. Omit superfluous matter and come to the point straight away. If you must refuse a request refuse it firmly without being blunt or impolite. Sometimes an idea if presented abruptly will upset or offend your reader, and in this case you should lead him gently into the subject.*
6 *Do not use terms you would not use outside business correspondence except to express a meaning more briefly when writing to people who understand the technical terminology of your business.*

Setting out a business letter

Whom to write to

Some companies and firms require letters to be addressed to them, rather than to individuals within the organization. An advantage of this system is that letters will still be dealt with if the person looking after the matter is away from the office. The normal opening for letters in such cases is 'Dear Sirs'.

Nowadays it is far more common to write to individuals and if you know your correspondent's name you should use it, checking that you have spelt it correctly of course. If you do not know the person's name you can write to 'The Sales Manager', 'The Managing Director' etc., beginning the letter 'Dear Sir'.

The heading

If you are replying to a letter with a heading, you should use the same heading in your reply and should quote a reference if one is given in the letter.

If you are writing what may be the first of a series of letters on a subject, it may be useful to use the same heading for each of them. You can also use a heading if it will considerably shorten your letter.

The opening paragraph

This should explain why you are writing the letter. If you are not using a heading this is where you should focus the reader's attention on the subject of your letter.

Do not use antiquated phrases like:

'We acknowledge receipt of', 'We are in receipt of', 'I have your letter of', 'we beg to acknowledge', 'your favour of 9th inst. to hand'. Use 'Thank you for' (not 'I' or 'We thank you for') or 'Many thanks for your letter of 8th March'. You might use 'You may remember writing to us on...' or 'Your letter of 5th May mentioned...'.

If you have spoken to your correspondent on the telephone you could write 'Thank you for your letter of 5th May and for telephoning me' or 'Thank you for your letter of 5th May. I also refer to our telephone conversation' or again 'With reference to your letter of 5th May and our subsequent telephone conversation'.

The body of the letter

Word the letter clearly and avoid ambiguous phrases. Avoid hackneyed expressions and 'commercialese'. Try not to use a long word where a short one would be just as accurate.

Avoid	**Use**
Ongoing	continuing
At the present time	
At this moment in time	now
At this juncture	
Currently	
Receive advices from	hear from
As advised in our letter	as stated in our letter
Your esteemed favour	your letter
Enclosed herewith	I am enclosing...
Beg	*Omit* unless you are a dog or a vagrant
Inform	let you know, mention, say, tell
Trust	hope
Renders	makes
Remit	pay or send
Ult., inst., prox.	give each month its name
The writer/the undersigned	I, me

Avoid at all costs such monstrosities as 'The present author opines'. 'I think' *would be so much better!*

To give an example of how these clichés can help to create a nonsense if used to excess, we have concocted a letter which appears to be guilty of all the faults imaginable.

'With reference to your esteemed favour of 20th ultimo and our reply thereto of the 9th instant, we hereby beg to advise that initial delivery will be actuated on 5th proximo with final delivery thereof to your goodselves on 11th idem.'

Full marks to anyone who can work out when any of these events was going to take place!

The final paragraph

You may wish to sum up the letter, or re-emphasize some point in it, in a final paragraph. Avoid old-fashioned phrases like 'Assuring you of our best attention at all times', 'Awaiting the favour of your esteemed command', 'Regretting our inability to be of service' or 'Trusting we may be favoured with the receipt' but end with a positive sentence like 'Please let us have your reply', 'what do you think?', 'do you agree?'. It is a good idea to end with a question as the reader will realize that you are expecting an answer from him.

Signing the letter

Use 'Yours faithfully' with 'Dear Sir' or 'Dear Sirs' and with 'Dear Madam', and 'Yours sincerely' for 'Dear Mr Jones' or other more personal salutations such as 'Dear Tony'.

Never sign letters with a rubber stamp. If a letter is worth writing it is worth signing by hand.

Read your letter carefully before sending it and check for mistakes. If your signature is difficult to decipher (and whose isn't?) type your name beneath it. Ladies might also put Mrs, Miss or Ms in brackets before their name.

If you are writing a letter for someone else sign your name 'for Sales Director', 'for Chief Education Officer', 'for Book Buyer'.

Forms of address for the commencement and conclusion of letters

The Sovereign

Address: To The Queen's Most Excellent Majesty.
Begin: Your Majesty; Madam; *or* May it please Your Majesty.
End: I have the honour to be, Your Majesty's most obedient subject and servant.

The Duke of Edinburgh

Address: To His Royal Highness the Duke of Edinburgh.
Begin: Your Royal Highness; *or* Sir.
End: I have the honour to be, Your Royal Highness' most obedient servant.

The Queen Mother

Address: To Her Majesty Queen Elizabeth the Queen Mother.
Begin: Your Majesty; Madam; *or* May it please Your Majesty.
End: I have the honour to be, Your Majesty's most obedient servant.

The Prince of Wales

Address: To His Royal Highness the Prince of Wales.
Begin: Your Royal Highness; *or* Sir.
End: I have the honour to be, Your Royal Highness' most obedient servant.

Royal Princes and Dukes

As for H.R.H. the Duke of Edinburgh.

Royal Princesses and Duchesses

Address: To Her Royal Highness the Princess Anne *or* To Her Royal Highness the Duchess of Kent.
Begin: Your Royal Highness; *or* Madam.
End: I have the honour to be, Your Royal Highness' most obedient servant.

A Duke or Duchess

Address: To His Grace the Duke of Barsetshire K.G. when a Knight of the Garter; K.T. when a Knight of the Thistle (or, Her Grace, the Duchess of Barsetshire).
Begin: My Lord Duke *or* Sir *or* Your Grace *or* Madam.
End: I have the honour to be, Your Grace's most obedient servant. The informal beginning and ending is 'Dear Duke' or 'Dear Duchess' and 'Yours sincerely'.

Duke's Children

The eldest son of a duke ranks as a peer by courtesy and is addressed as a Marquis or an Earl as the case may be, his sons being addressed as peer's sons.

Younger Sons of a Duke

Address: The Lord John Plantagenet.
Begin: My Lord; *or*, informally, Dear Lord John.
End: Your Lordship's most obedient servant; informally, Yours sincerely.

The Wife of a Duke's Younger Son

Address: The Lady John Plantagenet.
Begin: My Lady; or Dear Lady John.
End: Your Ladyship's most obedient servant; or, Yours sincerely.

Duke's Daughters (if unmarried)

Address: The Lady Mary Millington-Foster.
Begin: Madam; or Dear Lady Mary.
End: Your Ladyship's most obedient servant; or, Yours
sincerely.
N.B. If a Duke's daughter marries a Peer she assumes his
rank and is addressed as a Countess, etc. If she marries a
commoner, she continues to be addressed as the daughter
of a Duke, changing only her surname. For family surnames
of the members of the peerage, see Whitaker's Almanack.

Marquis or Marchioness

Address: To the Most Honourable the Marquis (or
Marchioness) of Steyne.
Begin: My Lord Marquis, or Sir, or Dear Lord Steyne;
or Madam, or Dear Lady Steyne.
End: Your Lordship's (or, Your Ladyship's) most obedient
servant; or, Yours sincerely.

CHILDREN OF A MARQUIS   The oldest son of a Marquis takes his
father's second title, and is addressed as a peer, his wife and
children as a peer's wife and children. Younger sons, and
daughters, of a Marquis, are given the title Lord or Lady as
for the children of Dukes.

Earl or Countess

Address: To the Right Hon. the Earl (or Countess) of
Camberley.
Begin: My Lord or Sir; My Lady or Madam; or, informally,
Dear Lord Camberley or Dear Lady Camberley.
End: Your Lordship's (or, Ladyship's) most obedient servant.
Or, Yours sincerely.

CHILDREN OF AN EARL   An Earl's eldest son ranks as a Viscount
and is addressed as such. Daughters and younger sons take

the title 'Honourable' used in place of 'Mr' or 'Miss'.

Address: The Hon. Freddy Finch-Fallow. The Hon. Jane
Finch-Fallow.

Begin: Dear Sir, or Dear Madam, or Dear Mr Finch-Fallow
or Dear Miss Finch-Fallow.

End: Yours faithfully, or Yours sincerely.

N.B. The daughter of an Earl who marries an untitled man
becomes 'The Hon. Mrs. Smith'. The wife of the son of an
Earl is 'The Hon. Mrs Freddy Finch-Fallow'.

Viscount or Viscountess

Address: To the Right Honourable the Viscount Milverton;
To the Right Honourable the Viscountess Milverton.

Begin: My Lord, Your Ladyship, Sir, or Madam. Informally,
Dear Lord Milverton, Dear Lady Milverton.

End: Your Lordship's (Ladyship's) obedient servant.
Informally, Yours sincerely.

Children of a Viscount

As for children of an Earl.

A Baron or Baroness

Address: To the Right Honourable the Lord Annesley; To
the Right Honourable the Lady Annesley, or
Baroness Annesley.

Begin and *End:* As for Viscount and Viscountess.

A BARONESS IN HER OWN RIGHT is addressed similarly to a lady
who is the wife of a Baron, and her children as a Baron's
children.

WIDOWS OF PEERS retain their title of 'Duchess',
'Countess', etc., so long as the next peer remains
unmarried, after which they become 'The Dowager
Duchess of Barsetshire'. 'The Dowager Marchioness of

Mercia', etc., if the mother or grandmother of the new peer. Of not so related to the new peer, the widow usually takes the title 'Mary, Duchess of Barsetshire', 'Anne, Marchioness of Mercia', etc. Beginnings and endings of letters, as for wives of peers.

Baronets and Knights and their Wives

Address: To Sir Norman Campbell, Bart. (or, Bt.); To Lady Campbell. To Sir Sidney Waterlow; To Lady Waterlow.
Begin: Sir; Dear Sir Norman; Dear Lady Campbell; Dear Sir Sidney; Dear Lady Waterlow; Madam.
End: Your obedient servant; Yours faithfully; Yours sincerely.

WIDOWS OF BARONETS become either The Dowager Lady Campbell or Lavinia, Lady Campbell, following the same rule as for widows of peers (q.v.). Letters to them begin and end in the same way as when their husbands were alive. Widows of knights continue to be addressed in the same way as when their husbands were alive.

Dames

Address: Dame Margaret Ferguson; *or,* Miss Margaret Ferguson, D.B.E.
Begin: Dear Dame Margaret; or, Madam.
End: Yours sincerely; Yours faithfully.

CHILDREN OF LIFE PEERS AND PEERESSES are addressed as private persons.

Private Persons

Address: James Smith, Esq.; or, Mr James Smith.
Begin: Dear Sir; or, Dear Mr Smith.
End: Yours faithfully; Yours sincerely; Yours truly.
N.B. Although strictly speaking Esquire is a title to which only certain people have the right (e.g. landed gentry, members of the bar, etc.) its use for all private gentlemen

as a matter of courtesy is sanctioned by modern custom, both in business and private correspondence.

Ladies

Address: Mrs James Smith or Mrs J. Smith; Miss Smith (if the eldest unmarried daughter); Miss Pamela Smith or Miss P. Smith if a younger unmarried daughter; Ms Smith.

Begin: Dear Madam, Dear Mrs Smith, Dear Miss Smith, Dear Ms Smith.

End: Yours faithfully; Yours sincerely; Yours truly.
N.B. The form 'Mrs Margaret Smith' or Mrs M. Smith' is used chiefly for divorcees and sometimes for women who have a business career in their own right.
Where two ladies have the same name, e.g., a mother-in-law and daughter-in-law who may both be Mrs James Smith, the younger may be addressed as Mrs James Smith, Jun. It is incorrect to address the older as Mrs James Smith, Sen.

Husband and Wife

Mr and Mrs Smith (no initials of degrees or professional qualifications).

Government and Other Officials
The Prime Minister

Address: The Right Hon. Alfred Winston, P.C., M.P., Prime Minister.

Begin: Dear Mr Prime Minister (Mrs, if a woman); Dear Mr Winston (Mrs, if a woman); Dear Sir Alfred (if a knight) or Lady Elizabeth (if a Lady); Dear Prime Minister (informal).

End: Yours faithfully; Yours sincerely.

Prime Ministers of Commonwealth Countries

Address: The Right Hon. John MacIlwray, P.C., M.P., Prime Minister of New Zealand.

Begin and *End* as for the British Prime Minister.

Members of the British Cabinet

Address: The Right Hon. Edward Cardwell, P.C., M.P.,
    Secretary of ——.
Begin: Dear Mr Cardwell.
End: Yours sincerely.

If a Woman

Address: The Right Hon. Ellen Bondfield, P.C., M.P.,
    Minister of Education
Begin: Dear Madam Minister; Dear Miss (or Mrs or Ms).
End: Yours faithfully; Yours sincerely.

The Speaker of the House of Commons

Address: To the Right Hon. James Fotherington, Speaker of
    the House of Commons.
Begin: Sir; Dear Mr Speaker.
End: Your obedient servant; Yours faithfully; Yours sincerely.

Privy Councillors

All Privy Councillors, other than Dukes and Marquesses,
    have the title Right Honourable. In practice this is
    used, in correspondence, only in addressing those who have
    no other title.

Member of Parliament

Address: The Right Hon. Peter Smith, P.C.; The Right Hon.
    Edith Brown, P.C.
Begin: Dear Sir; Dear Mr Smith; Dear Madam; Madam;
    Dear Miss Brown.
End: Yours faithfully; Yours sincerely.
If titled, address according to rank; begin and end letter
    accordingly. If untitled, address as a private person, with
    the addition of the letters M.P. after the address.
    Beginning and end of letter, as for private person.

Governor-General

Address: To His Excellency Sir Edward Jones, Governor-General of Australia. (Or, Lord Jones, or according to rank.)

Begin: Your Excellency; Dear Governor-General; Dear Sir Edward (or, Dear Lord Jones).

End: Your Excellency's obedient servant; Yours faithfully; Yours sincerely.

Ambassadors

Address: To His Excellency the Right Hon. Michael Murdoch (or, The Earl of Murdoch, etc., according to rank); Her Britannic Majesty's Ambassador.

Begin: Your Excellency; Sir; Dear Lord Murdoch (or, according to rank).

End: Your Excellency's obedient servant; Yours faithfully; Yours sincerely.

Ministers, Envoys, Consuls, Legation Secretaries

Address: Henry Brown, Esq. (or according to rank); Her Britannic Majesty's Minister (or, Consul, or Secretary to the Legation).

Begin and *End:* As for private individuals or according to rank.

Commonwealth Privy Councillors

As Privy Councillors of Great Britain, except that the title is 'The Honourable', not 'The Right Honourable'.

THE WIVES OF THE ABOVE OFFICIALS are addressed according to their private rank, *not* with reference to their husband's official position.

Clergymen
Archbishop

Address: To His Grace the Lord Archbishop of Canterbury.
Begin: My Lord Archbishop; Your Grace; Dear Lord
  Archbishop (informal).
End: Your Lordship's obedient servant; Yours respectfully;
  Yours sincerely.

Bishops

Address: To the Right Reverend the Lord Bishop of
  Barchester.
Begin: My Lord Bishop; Dear Bishop (informal).
End: Your most obedient servant; Yours faithfully;
  Yours sincerely.

Roman Catholic Bishops and Archbishops

Address: His Excellency the Most Reverend Michael
  O'Flaherty, Archbishop (or Bishop) of ——.
Begin: Your Excellency; Dear Archbishop; Dear Bishop.
End: Your Excellency's Most obedient servant; Yours
  respectfully; Yours sincerely.

SCOTTISH BISHOPS are addressed personally as Right Rev.
  Bishop Mackenzie, D.D.; *not* The Right Rev. the Lord
  Bishop of Glamis.

Deans and Archdeacons

Address: To the Very Reverend the Dean of Barchester;
  To the Venerable the Archdeacon.
Begin: Very Reverend Sir; Dear Dean; Venerable Sir;
  Dear Archdeacon.
End: Your obedient servant; Yours faithfully; Yours sincerely.

Canon

Address: The Rev. Canon Browne, D.D.
Begin: Reverend Sir; Dear Canon; Dear Canon Browne.
End: Your obedient servant; Yours faithfully; Yours sincerely.

Clergymen and Ministers, if with a Doctor's Degree

Address: The Rev. James Chasuble, D.D.
Begin: Dear Dr Chasuble; Dear Rector; Dear Vicar;
   Dear Sir.
End: Yours sincerely; Yours faithfully.

If without a Doctor's Degree

Address: The Rev. John Phillips, B.A.
Begin: Dear Mr Phillips; Dear Rector; Dear Vicar;
   Dear Father Phillips; Dear Sir.
End: Yours sincerely; Yours faithfully.

Jewish Rabbi

Address: Rabbi Aaron Joseph.
Begin: Dear Rabbi Joseph; Dear Rabbi.
End: Yours sincerely; Yours faithfully.

THE WIVES OF CLERGYMEN are invariably addressed by their
   private rank, not according to their husband's office.
   E.g., although a Bishop may be addressed as 'My Lord
   Bishop' his wife will still be addressed as 'Dear Mrs
   Proudie' or 'Dear Madam', unless she happens to have a
   title in her own right.

CLERGYMEN WHO HAVE TITLES OF SECULAR RANK as well as
   their church title, are addressed by both, the church title
   being put first. Thus, the son of a Duke who became a
   curate would be addressed as The Rev. Lord James
   Jernigan; the son of an Earl would be The Rev. The Hon.
   John Morrell. Begin and end letters as for the sons of

peers. Their wives are addressed by the secular rank only, Lady James Jernigan or The Hon. Mrs John Morrell.

Officers of the Services

Address: with titles according to rank. Admiral Lord Hornblower, K.G.; or General Sir William Everett, K.C.M.G.; Captain, *or* Commander, Hardy, R.N.; Major William Jones, V.C.; Lieutenant Andrews, R.N.; Group Captain T. Shaw, R.A.F.
It is usual to add after the officer's name either the letters R.N. or R.A.F., or, if in the army, the initials or name of his regiment, e.g., R.A. or R.E.; these initials come *before* any decorations or distinctions such as V.C., D.S.O., etc.

Begin: Sir; Dear Captain Andrews.

End: I am, sir, your obedient servant; Yours faithfully; Yours sincerely.

WIVES OF OFFICERS are addressed by their private rank; e.g., an Admiral's wife will be Mrs Hornblower, unless she has rank of her own, e.g., Lady Barbara Hornblower.

The Medical Profession

Address: Dr S. Palmer or S. Palmer, Esq., M.D.

Begin: Dear Sir; Dear Dr Palmer.

End: Yours faithfully; Yours sincerely.

N.B. Surgeons are addressed as Mr or Mrs *not* Dr, and S. Palmer Esq., M.R.C.S. on the envelope for men and Miss/Mrs/Ms V. Dean M.R.C.S. for women.

The Lord Chancellor

Address: To the Right Honourable the Lord High Chancellor of England.

Begin: My Lord Chancellor; My Lord; Dear Lord Whigham (informal).

End: Your Lordship's obedient servant; Yours sincerely.

Lord Chief Justice

Address: To the Right Honourable the Lord Chief Justice of
England; or To the Right Honourable Lord Burkhill,
Lord Chief Justice of England (according to rank).
Begin: My Lord; Sir; Dear Lord Burkhill.
End: Your Lordship's obedient servant; Yours sincerely.

The Lord Advocate (Scotland)

Address: To the Right Honourable the Lord Advocate;
or To the Right Honourable James Burns, Lord Advocate.
Begin: Sir; Dear Lord Advocate.
End: Your obedient Servant; Yours faithfully; Yours
sincerely.

Lord Justice of Appeal

Address: To the Right Hon. Lord Justice Simpson.
Begin: My Lord; Sir; Dear Lord Simpson *or* Dear Sir John
(according to rank).
End: Your obedient servant; Yours faithfully; Yours
sincerely.

High Court Judge

Address: To the Honourable Mr Justice Benson.
Begin: Sir; Dear Sir, Dear Mr Justice Benson.
If a woman
Address: To the Honourable Mrs Justice Clark.
Begin: Madam; Dear Madam; Dear Dame
Mary Clark.
End: Your obedient servant; Yours faithfully; Yours
sincerely.

County Court Judge

Address: To His Honour Judge Warner.
Begin: Your Honour; Sir; Dear Judge Warner.
If a woman
Address: To Her Honour Judge Jones.
Begin: Your Honour, Madam; Dear Judge Jones.
End: As for High Court Judge.

Lord Mayor

Address: The Right Honourable the Lord Mayor of
   Barchester; *or* The Right Hon. Sir Arthur Beecham,
   Lord Mayor of Barchester.
Begin and *End:* as for a Baron.

Mayor

Address: The Worshipful the Mayor of Silchester.
Begin: Your Worship; Sir; Dear Mr Mayor.
End: Yours faithfully; Yours sincerely.

THE WIFE OF A MAYOR or Lord Mayor is the Mayoress
   or Lady Mayoress. She is not addressed as 'Right
   Honourable' or 'Worshipful'. Letters to her begin
   'Madam', 'Dear Lady Mayoress' or 'Dear Madam
   Mayoress' and end as for the Mayor.

A WOMAN MAYOR is addressed exactly as a man Mayor.
   Letters to her begin 'Madam', 'Your Worship', 'Dear
   Madam Mayor' or, occasionally, 'Dear Mr Mayor'.
   Never use the word 'Mayoress' for a woman Mayor.

Model letters

Formal invitations

Formal wedding invitation, sent by parents of bride

Mr and Mrs Martin Thompson
request the pleasure of
the company of
Mr and Mrs B. Jameson
at the marriage of their daughter
Susan Alice
to
Mr Henry Arkwright
at
St Mark's Church, Bearstow Heath,
on Wednesday 6th June at 3 p.m.
and afterwards at the Jolly Woodmen,
Knightwell.

12 Seymour Street,   R.S.V.P.
Bearstow Heath,
Greater Manchester.

Where the bridegroom is titled, or is a doctor, clergyman or officer in the Services, his title is given on the wedding invitation. It is normal to use any decorations he has won but not to indicate degrees or professional qualifications.

Normally wedding invitations are sent by the bride's parents and when they are not the hosts the invitation should make clear the relationship between the hosts and the bride.

Wedding Invitation when the bride's parents are not the hosts

Mr and Mrs Martin Thompson
request the pleasure of
the company of
Mr and Mrs B. Jameson
at the marriage of their niece
Catherine Barton
to
Mr. James Mitchell
etc.

Wedding invitation from step-parents

Mr and Mrs Joseph Hoyle
request the pleasure of
the company of
Phillip Marsden
at the marriage of
Mr Hoyle's daughter
Anne
etc.

Acceptance of formal wedding invitation

4 Ashwin Gardens,
Bearstow Heath.

Mr and Mrs Bernard Jameson have much pleasure in accepting
Mr and Mrs Martin Thompson's kind invitation to the
marriage of their daughter Susan on Wednesday 6th June.

28th April 19—

Declining invitation to wedding

> 4 Ashwin Gardens,
> Bearstow Heath.

Mr and Mrs Bernard Jameson much regret that they are
unable to accept Mr and Mrs Martin Thompson's kind
invitation to the marriage of their daughter on 6th June, as
they will be on holiday abroad.

> 28th April 19—

Recalling wedding invitation

Mr and Mrs Barnaby Smith announce that the marriage of
their daughter Elizabeth to Dr Andrew Warner will not
now take place.

Postponement of wedding invitation

> Mr and Mrs Richard Truman
> announce that owing to the illness of Mr Jenkins
> the marriage of their daughter
> Barbara
> to
> Mr Phillip Jenkins
> has been postponed indefinitely.

4 Mount Place, Reading.

Cancellation of wedding invitation because of family mourning

Mr and Mrs Bruce Richardson
regret exceedingly
that owing to the recent death of
the father of Mr Richardson
the invitations to the marriage of their daughter
Pamela
to
Dr Paul Ellis
must be cancelled.

82 Alice Road,
Warwick.

Formal invitation to dinner

Mr and Mrs Smith request the pleasure of the company of
Mr and Mrs Evans at dinner on Wednesday, October 16th
at 7.30 for 8 o'clock.

9 King's Road, Brecon, Powys.
Monday 31st September

Invitation using a printed 'At Home' card

Mrs Angela Lawrence
AT HOME
Friday, 28th October
8 o'clock

Fork buffet

R.S.V.P.
17 Albany Street,
Hereford.

Formal invitations to dances, bridge parties, garden parties, etc.

These follow the form of AT HOME invitations, the word 'Dancing', 'Bridge', etc. being added in the left-hand bottom corner. The forms of acceptance and refusal are as for formal invitations to weddings.

Announcements

Engagement announcement in newspaper

ROGERS – PINTER. The engagement is announced between Raymond, only son of Mr and Mrs William Rogers of Boscombe, Bournemouth and Angela Mary, elder daughter of Mr and Mrs Frank Pinter of Davenport, Cheshire.

Announcement in newspaper of forthcoming marriage

Mr G. Glover and Miss S. Williams
The marriage arranged between Mr George Glover and Miss Sarah Williams will take place at All Saints Church, Ford Green on Wednesday, March 20th at 3 p.m. Friends will be welcome at the church.

Marriage announcement in newspaper

WHITE – BROOKS. On 27th June 19— at St Michael's Church, Lynton, Richard, son of Mrs S. White and the late Mr E. H. White of London and Sarah, younger daughter of Doctor and Mrs W. Brooks of Lynton.

Marriage announcement

The marriage took place yesterday at St Mary's Church, Wilhame between the Rev. James Gordon Codrington of Sheffield, Yorkshire and Mrs Margaret Joan Hutchinson of Wilhame, Hampshire, daughter of Mrs Janet Fowler and the late Mr Harold Fowler, and widow of Mr Edward Hutchinson.

Death announcement in newspaper

JACOBS – on 9th March 19—, Ann Elizabeth, wife of the late Mark Jacobs and mother of Marion and Alexander. Service and cremation at West Park Crematorium on Friday at 11 a.m. Enquiries to Allen Brothers, Funeral Directors, 23 High St, West Park.

In Memoriam notice in newspaper

WILSON – Birthday memories of Veronica, the dearly loved wife of Patrick.

Announcement of wedding anniversary

BENTLEY : PATERSON. On 25th June 19— (date of wedding) at St Paul's Church, Bath, Lieutenant Michael Paul Bentley R.N. to Elizabeth Mary Paterson. Present address: Lavender House, Havant, Hants.

Birth announcement in newspaper

MASTERS On August 14th in Cardiff, to Mary (née Brewer) and Peter, a daughter Isabel Jane, a sister for Anthony and Paul.

Adoption announcement in newspaper

FISHER. – By Sarah (née Humphreys) and Michael Fisher – a son James Matthew, now aged $8\frac{1}{2}$ months.

Newspaper announcement acknowledging thanks for sympathy

CHARRINGTON. The family of the late Nigel Charrington wish to express their sincere thanks to all relatives, friends and business associates for their kindness, expressions of sympathy and for the flowers received. Thanks also to the doctors and staff of the Paddock Bourne Hospital.

Engagement and marriage

**Letter to a friend announcing forthcoming marriage
 or engagement (1)**

9 The Crescent,
Gillamoor,
North Yorkshire.

25th October 19—

Dear Helen,

I am sure you will be glad to hear that Andrew and I
have decided to get married and have fixed our wedding for
3rd December. We are getting married at St Mary's Church
and my mother is making my dress. Andrew and I have found
a flat near here and are busy decorating it and choosing
furniture.

As you can imagine, I am terribly busy at the moment and
don't know which way to turn next.

I do hope you are all keeping well. Please give my regards
to your parents.

With love,

Letter to a friend announcing forthcoming marriage or engagement (2)

19 Greenway Avenue,
Fontwell,
West Sussex.

27th March 19—

My dear Bill,

I wanted to let you know that I am getting married again. I am sure you will realize how lonely I have been since Mary died two years ago and though I will always miss her I am sure she would not want me to remain a widower all my life.

My fiancée, Susan Hillier, is a journalist. We have known each other for about a year now and are planning a very quiet wedding some time in the summer.

I do hope to see you again soon and to introduce you to Susan.

Yours ever,

Letter to a prospective son-in-law

9 Grange Road,
West Felton,
Salop.

9 July 19—

My dear Howard,

Jennifer has written telling us of your engagement and although we shall be seeing you both at the weekend I felt I must write at once to tell you how happy my husband and I are at this news. There is nobody we would rather have as a son-in-law than you and we welcome the closer link that this will mean with your own family. After being friends for so long, we are now actually to be related.

I am writing to your mother and hope that she and Mr Evans will be able to come over for lunch on Saturday as I'm sure we shall all have a lot to talk about then.

Yours affectionately,

Letter to a prospective daughter-in-law

19 Ross Road,
Hereford.

10th July 19—

My dear Jennifer,

Howard has told me of your engagement and although I hope to see you very soon, I must write at once to tell you how pleased my husband and I are, and how happy it has made us.

We very much hope that Howard will bring you to see us quite soon as we are greatly looking forward to hearing more about your future plans and welcoming you to our family as a prospective daughter-in-law.

We both send our love and every good wish for your future happiness.

Yours sincerely,

Letter to prospective parents-in-law

8 Pennyworth Road,
Chelmsford,
Essex.

19 May 19—

Dear Mr and Mrs Harper,

I have just received Mrs Harper's very sweet letter and wanted to thank you for your good wishes. I have heard so much about you both and am looking forward to meeting you and to showing you the beautiful ring Tom has just bought me.

Yours affectionately,

Letter from one set of prospective in-laws to the other

9 Grange Road,
West Felton,
Salop.

9th July 19—

Dear Mrs Evans,

I am sure by now you have heard from Howard of his engagement to Jennifer – not that it was exactly a surprise to us, and no doubt you, too, were waiting for the announcement.

John and I are are so happy about it; we have grown very fond of Howard. He is just the kind of son we would have liked to have ourselves.

Jennifer and Howard are coming over here to stay at the weekend and we would all be very pleased if you and

Mr Evans could come over for the day on Saturday. I am sure we shall all have plenty to talk about.

With kindest regards to yourself and Mr Evans.

Yours sincerely,

Reply to above

19 Ross Road,
Hereford.

Dear Mrs West,

Thank you for your kind letter. My husband and I have realized for some time how much Jennifer means to Howard and were very happy to learn of their engagement. We have grown very attached to Jennifer and are looking forward to meeting her family. It is very kind of you to invite us over on Saturday and we are delighted to accept.

Yours sincerely,

Letter of congratulation on an engagement

8 Lyfield Way,
Market Harborough,
Leics.

7th February 19—

My dear Mike,

I have just seen the announcement in the Telegraph of your engagement to Sally Jones and I wanted to send you my congratulations. Sally is a charming girl and I am sure you will both be very happy together.

Yours ever,

Letter to a friend upon the breaking of an engagement

8 East Mews,
Weymouth Street,
London WIM 2LB,

7th July 19—

Dear Phillip,

I have just seen the announcement in the paper of the breaking off of your engagement. This kind of thing is bound to be pretty painful and embarrassing and there isn't much one can say to help matters.

If it would help to drop in for a chat any time, we are in most evenings.

Yours,

Informal wedding invitation (1)

3 Abbeydale Road,
Sidmouth,
Devon.

4th March 19—

Dear Mr and Mrs Mount,

Our daughter Jill is to be married on Wednesday 5th May to Mr Paul Williams. It would give us great pleasure if you could attend the wedding, which will be at St Mary's Church, The Green, at 2.30 p.m. As Paul's father has recently died the wedding will be a very quiet one and we will be inviting only close friends. We hope you will be able to come back for tea after the ceremony.

Yours sincerely,

Informal wedding invitation (2)

10 Valentine Road,
Buxton.

7th November 19—

Dear Mary,

It'll be no surprise to you to hear that James and I are getting married. The ceremony will be at 11.45 a.m. on 30th November at Buxton Register Office, and we both very much hope you will be able to come. We are inviting only about a dozen close friends and we hope that everyone will join us for lunch.

With love from both of us,

Letter to a friend, asking her to be a bridesmaid

*Traditionally the bride will ask first her own sisters and then
her bridegroom's sisters to act as bridesmaids. Only after these
should she invite friends or more distant relatives. Only
unmarried girls can be bridesmaids, but a married sister or friend
can be invited to attend as Matron of Honour.*

15 The Poplars,
Cambridge.

4th January 19—

Dear Louise,

As you know George and I have fixed our wedding for
20th March at All Saints Church, Ford Green. I would be
so pleased if you would be one of my bridesmaids. George's
sister, whom I think you have met, is to be the other
bridesmaid. I, of course, have only brothers.

We have not yet settled on dresses but as soon as I hear that
you are able to be a bridesmaid I will discuss the dresses
with you.

With love,

Letter to a friend, asking him to act as best man

18 Wells Way,
York.

10th June 19—

Dear Tom,

   As you know Penny and I are getting married on 20th July
and I am writing to ask you a great favour: would you act
as my best man? You have been a good friend for so long,
there is nobody I would rather have around to support me.
Penny is very fond of you too, and wants to introduce you to
the bridesmaids!

Yours ever,

Letter of thanks for wedding present

9 Arndale Rise,
Cuffley,
Herts.

7th June 19—

Dear Mary,

Tom and I thank you so much for your lovely gift. A wine rack
is one of the things we very much wanted and no-one but you
was clever enough to think of it.

   We got home from our honeymoon on Friday and are
now getting the house in order. There is so much to be done
but the rooms are beginning to take shape at last.

   We both hope you will come and see us in the
not-too-distant future.

   Again many thanks and every good wish from us both.

Yours affectionately,

Letter of thanks after a wedding

19 Dolphin Close,
Charfield,
Avon.

15th August 19—

Dear Mrs Butler,

This is to say how pleased I was to be able to attend the wedding on Saturday. Mary really looked lovely and you could not have wished for a sunnier day.

I really enjoyed every minute of the reception as well. You really made all your guests feel welcome and Mr Butler certainly missed his vocation as a speaker. Thank you so much for inviting me.

Yours sincerely,

Letter returning engagement or wedding present, as the wedding will not now take place

23 Hemming Way,
Dundee.

8th April 19—

Dear Louise,

You may already have heard that David and I have decided not to get married. As you can imagine this was a very difficult decision for both of us but we are sure it is the right one. It is best that we have both found out our true feelings now rather than later.

In the circumstances we feel it is only fair to return the gift you so very kindly sent us.

Yours affectionately,

Birth and adoption

Letter announcing the birth of a child

Elm Lodge,
Bainbridge Way,
Cardiff.

16th August 19—

Dear George,

I am delighted to tell you that Mary had a daughter on
Friday morning at 8.30. She weighed seven and a half pounds
at birth and has a mop of black hair. We have decided to
call her Isabel after my grandmother. Both mother and child
are doing very well, I'm glad to say, and we all look forward
to seeing you soon.

Yours ever,

Reply to above

8 Elm Road,
Harrogate.

18th August 19—

Dear Mary and Peter,

I have just received your letter and am delighted to hear
the wonderful news. Please accept my sincere congratulations
upon the birth of Isabel. I am so very glad for you both. I am
sure the boys must be very proud of their little sister.

I hope very much to be able to come and see you all soon and
congratulate you in person.

Yours ever,

Letter of congratulation on the birth of a child

208 Brock Way,
Holland Park,
w8k 5ww.

16th October 19—

My dear Alice,

Please accept my sincere congratulations to you and Dick on the birth of a son. It was the one thing needed to complete your lives together. As an old bachelor, I realize strongly how much the world owes to the parents of beautiful children – without them it would be about as cheerful as a garden without flowers! Your little son will, I feel sure, bring you ever increasing happiness in the years ahead.

I am delighted to hear from your mother that you are both getting on so well.

With love from your son's proud great uncle,

Letter of congratulation on the adoption of a child

238 Charles Street,
London NW3 4BT.

21st July 19—

Dear Tom and Valerie,

I have just heard your good news. I know how much you have both wished for this and how happy your new son will make you. I look forward to meeting him soon.

Yours sincerely,

Condolence and Bereavement

**Letter from a widow, informing her husband's
employers of his death**

> 7 Mount Street,
> Bury St Edmunds,
> Suffolk.
>
> 9th December 19—

Dear Sirs,

I am writing to inform you that my husband died suddenly
in the early hours of this morning. Please excuse this very
short note. As you can imagine I am greatly shocked but
will write to you more fully as soon as I am able.

Yours faithfully,

From a lady to a relative, informing him of her husband's death and requesting assistance

7 Mount Street,
Bury St Edmunds,
Suffolk.

9th December 19—

My dear Bill,

You will have had my telegram telling you that Brian died suddenly this morning. I should be more than grateful if you could spare the time to come and help me with the arrangements. There is a great deal to be looked after and I do not feel up to giving the necessary instructions for the funeral.

Of course I shall understand if you cannot manage to come.

Yours very affectionately,

Letter to a relative, asking him to attend a funeral

15 Ladbroke Road,
Broadstairs,
Kent.

8th June 19—

My dear Uncle Bob,

You will have heard of father's sudden death yesterday morning. Mother is of course extremely distressed and is unable to write to you or telephone you herself but she would like me to say that she hopes you will be able to attend the funeral on Friday next at 2.30 p.m. at Northfields Cemetery.

With fondest love,

Letter announcing a death to a friend

8 Maybury Court,
Standish Road,
York.

7th May 19—

Dear Mrs Andrews,

You will be sorry to learn that my mother passed away on Monday. She was only ill for a week and as you can imagine we are all very shocked. The funeral will be at St Mary's on 10th May at 3 p.m.

Yours sincerely,

Letter of condolence to the widow of a former employee

Turner, Robinson and Co.,
11 Banbury Rd.,
Reading, Berks.

11th November 19—

Dear Mrs Howard,

It was with a sense of shock and sorrow that I learned of the death of your husband and I know that these feelings are shared by all who knew him and worked with him during his years with this firm.

Please accept the sincere sympathy of all your husband's former colleagues here, and of myself personally.

Yours sincerely,

Reply to above

'The Pines',
9 Marchmont Avenue,
Reading, Berks.

14th November 19—

Dear Mr Turner,

Thank you for your letter on behalf of yourself and the firm. I am still feeling very stunned and bewildered by my husband's death. I am glad to say his illness was very short and he did not suffer greatly.

My husband often spoke of his days with your firm as being one of the happiest periods of his life and would be pleased to know his former colleagues still remember him.

Thank you once again for your kind expression of sympathy.

Yours sincerely,

Letter of condolence (more distant)

6 Wicks Crescent,
Hexham.

9th March 19—

Dear Mrs King,

My wife and I were extremely sad to read in the 'Gazette' of your husband's sudden death. There is little one can say at such a time but we would both like to express our very sincere sympathy to you. If there is any way in which we can be of practical assistance, please do let us know.

Yours sincerely,

Reply to the above letter

9 Sheldon Drive,
Chester.

14th November 19—

Dear Mr James,

Thank you for your kind letter. The death of my husband
has been an enormous shock and it is a great help to know that
friends are thinking of me.

Yours sincerely,

Letter to a friend who has just been divorced

29 Beverley Terrace,
Manchester 2.

28th June 19—

Dear Mary,

John and I heard yesterday that your divorce has just
come through. I am sure it must feel strange to be single again
after all these years but at the same time it must be quite
exciting to be starting a completely new life.

If there is anything we can do, please do not hesitate to
phone or to come round. If you would like to come and stay
with us for a week or so you know you are very welcome.

With love,

Letter to a friend in financial difficulties, enclosing a cheque

9 Riverside Walk,
Gloucester.

My dear Susan,

I know that Bill's long illness must be a very great strain on your resources and I hope you will not be offended in any way by the enclosed cheque. It will give me great pleasure to help you a little and I hope you'll accept this small gift and use the money in whatever way you think best.

I do hope Bill has taken a real turn for the better now and that he will soon be completely fit again.

The family joins me in sending you both our best love.

Yours affectionately,

Letter to a friend ill in hospital (1)

9 Courtland Way,
Holmfirth,
W. Yorks.

20th December 19—

Dear Josephine,

I am sending you some fruit with my very best wishes for a quick recovery. What bad luck that you should be admitted to hospital just before Christmas – still the main thing is to find out what is wrong and to get strong and well again.

With much love,

Letter to a friend ill in hospital (2)

8 Cottingham Place,
Meriden,
W. Midlands.

18th July 19—

Dear Marion,

We were all so sorry to hear you are in hospital and that you will have to undergo an operation. I know you have been feeling ill for a month or so and I do hope that your stay in hospital will put things right. We are all thinking of you and looking forward to hearing that you are getting better.

With all good wishes for a very speedy return to health.

Yours affectionately,

Letter offering help to a friend in trouble

17 Bell Grove,
Lancaster.

29th April 19—

Dear Tom,

I was very sorry to hear of the fire at your house and I understand that the bedrooms are badly damaged. How lucky none of you were hurt.

I am sure you must be very busy clearing up the mess and if there is anything I can do to help, please let me know. Do write and let us know what you are doing because we have plenty of room if you would like to come and stay with us for a while or if you prefer to stay at your house we could lend you a camp bed and some bedding. Just let me know if we can be of assistance, otherwise don't trouble to reply yet as you must be extremely busy.

Yours ever,

Letters of congratulations

Letter of congratulations upon an 18th or 21st birthday

7 St Andrew's Grove,
Bromley, Kent.

20th January 19—

Dear Christine,

I send all my good wishes and thoughts for this important day. I am sure you are terribly excited and that you are busy preparing for your party this evening. I do hope it will be a huge success and that everyone will have a good time. I only wish I could be with you.

Much love and every good wish for the future.

Yours affectionately,

Congratulations note, to enclose with 18th or 21st birthday present

From Jack and Mary Morris to Simon, with best wishes for today and for the future on this his eighteenth (twenty-first) birthday.

22nd January 19—

Letter of congratulations to a friend upon his son's or daughter's success

19 Combe Crescent,
Exeter.

16th May 19—

Dear Bill,

Allow me to congratulate you upon Anthony's success in passing his final examinations. You must all be glad that his time of study and anxiety is over. It is good to hear of a son who repays by hard work and success all the care his parents have put into his education.

Yours sincerely,

Letter of congratulations upon a professional success

7 Vicarage Gardens,
Worcester.

7th May 19—

Dear Robin,

It was with great pleasure that I read in the paper this morning of your appointment to the Board of Taylor Machines Ltd. This is a marvellous achievement, though no more than you deserve. Please accept my heartiest congratulations and best wishes for the future.

Yours sincerely,

Letter of congratulation on passing an examination

92 Maytime Park,
Darlington.

19th August 19—

Dear Tony,

I was delighted to hear that you passed your examination.
Congratulations! I know you worked very hard indeed and it
would have been most unfair if you had not passed with
flying colours.

Every good wish for your career ahead.

Yours sincerely,

Social correspondence

Letter inviting a friend to stay

Merrow House,
169 Dale Road,
Bristol 7,
Avon.

8th August 19—

Dear Louise,

It seems ages since we saw you and I wonder if you are free
to visit us the weekend after next. The garden is looking
very pretty just now and it would be very pleasant if you
could come while the fine weather holds. Bring your
swimming costume as we go swimming nearly every day.
Let me know if we can expect you.

Much love,

Reply accepting above

84 Willow Tree Hill,
Highgate,
London N6B 5JY.

11th August 19—

Dear Barbara,

Thank you for your letter. It is very kind of you to invite
me for the weekend of 23rd August and I would love to
come. I shall come down by the train which arrives at
Temple Meads Station at 2.35 p.m., but please do not trouble
to meet the train as I know my way from the station
quite well.

Yours affectionately,

Reply declining

84 Willow Tree Hill,
Highgate,
London N6B 5JY.

11th August 19—

Dear Barbara,

Thank you for your letter and for your kind invitation to
stay. Unfortunately, I have to work on alternate Saturdays
now and shall not be able to get away. I am very
disappointed, as I would have loved to see you all again, but I
am afraid it cannot be helped.

Yours affectionately,

Letter of thanks for a visit

84 Willow Tree Hill,
Highgate,
London N6B 5JY.

27th August 19—

Dear Barbara,

Just a line to let you know that I arrived home safely after a very pleasant train journey.

Thank you so much for a delightful weekend. I really enjoyed every minute of it. I shall remember the picnic in the woods for a long time to come – especially the delicious lemon soufflé you made! It was marvellous to see you again and to have a really long chat.

Yours affectionately,

Informal invitation to a supper party

19 Peals Row,
Hampstead,
London NW3 5TL.

8th September 19—

Dear Bill and Mary,

We are having a small supper party here on 15th September to celebrate Sarah's birthday and we would be so pleased if you could join us at about 8 p.m. Come as you are.

Yours sincerely,

Letter of thanks after a dinner party

7 New Road,
Gateshead,
Tyne and Wear.

4th December 19—

Dear Jane,

This is to thank you so much for inviting me round for dinner on Friday. It was a wonderful evening and I really enjoyed myself. It was a great pleasure to meet some of your friends and I also enjoyed the delicious meal. You certainly are an excellent cook and hostess.

Yours sincerely,

Invitation to a children's party

Invitations for very small children are usually sent on the small illustrated cards to be bought from most stationers. Alternative forms, to be written by hand, are given below. It is a good idea to set a time for the party to end, so that parents can arrange to collect their children and take them home.

7 Lansdowne Road,
Skipton,
North Yorkshire.

27th March 19—

Dear Mrs Steele,

Would Rosemary and Tom be able to come to a children's tea-party in our house on 5th April from four o'clock until six? It is Michael's birthday and we thought it would be a good idea to have a small party for him.

Yours sincerely,

Reply accepting above

19 Lansdowne Road,
Skipton,
North Yorkshire.

30th March 19—

Dear Mrs Baker,

Thank you for your kind invitation. Rosemary and Tom
would love to come to Michael's birthday party and are
already very excited about it. They will come down to you at
four and I will come to collect them at six.
With many thanks.

Yours sincerely,

Reply declining above

19 Lansdowne Road,
Skipton,
North Yorkshire.

30th March 19—

Dear Mrs Baker,

Thank you for your kind invitation to Rosemary and Tom.
Unfortunately they have both got rather heavy colds and as
I would not like the other children to catch their germs
I must refuse. We all hope Michael will have a lovely party
and enjoy his birthday. Please wish him many happy returns
of the day.

Yours sincerely,

Thanks afterwards

19 Lansdowne Road,
Skipton,
North Yorkshire.

7th April 19—

Dear Mrs Baker,

Rosemary and Tom so much enjoyed the party on
Saturday and came home full of stories about the games
they played and the wonderful tea you had prepared. Thank
you so much for inviting them.

Yours sincerely,

Children's education

Letter enquiring about a school

9 Waverley Avenue,
London sw18 9ju.

The Principal,
St George's School,
Southampton.

7th April 19—

Dear Sir,

My husband and I are at present considering the
alternatives for the education of our son of thirteen and
would like to discuss with you the possibility that he might
become a boarder at St George's. Would you please send us
a prospectus of the school and let us have details of your terms.

Before finally arriving at a decision we would like to see
the school for ourselves and know more about various points
which really need personal discussion, such as the size of

class, what outside examinations the children are prepared for and which languages are taught. Would you please let us know when it would be convenient for us to come down to see you.

Yours faithfully,

Acknowledging the principal's reply

9 Waverley Avenue,
London sw18 9ju.

The Principal,
St George's School,
Southampton.

12th April 19—

Dear Sir,

Thank you for your letter of 10th April and for the prospectus. We would like to bring our son down to see the school on Monday of next week and will come to your office at 3 p.m. as you suggest.

Yours faithfully,

Entering a child for school

9 Waverley Avenue,
London sw18 9ju.

J. Sinclair Esq., MA,
St George's School,
Southampton.   20th April 19—

Dear Mr Sinclair,

   Thank you for your letter of 17th April. I am delighted
to learn that James has passed the Entrance Examination and
that you will accept him as a pupil. I am returning the
completed Entrance Form together with my cheque for the
first term's fees, including the extra amount payable for
piano lessons. No doubt you will be letting me know shortly
what uniform and sports equipment James will need and the
names of the school outfitters.

Yours sincerely,

Letter to a headmaster about pupil's inattention
   at school

9 Waverley Avenue,
London sw18 9ju.

J. Sinclair Esq., MA,
St George's School,
Southampton.   17th September 19—

Dear Mr Sinclair,

   Thank you for your letter of 15th September. Although it
caused me concern I am very grateful to you for raising the
matter of my son's behaviour at school.

   James is coming home for the weekend very soon and
I will be having a serious talk with him, but in the meantime I

am sending him a letter pointing out that if he does not make a real effort to work harder he will certainly fail his examinations.

I do hope you will find an improvement in his work from now on and I would be very grateful if you could keep me informed of his progress.

Yours sincerely,

Letter to a headmaster, asking that a pupil might take an extra subject

9 Waverley Avenue,
London sw18 9ju.

J. Sinclair Esq., MA,
St George's School,
Southampton.   17th September 19—

Dear Mr Sinclair,

Would it be possible for my son James to take violin lessons? He is as you know very gifted musically and his grandmother has agreed to buy him a violin if he promises to practise regularly.

I look forward to hearing from you if this can be arranged and what the extra cost will be.

Yours sincerely,

Letter to a Headmistress, about a backward pupil

6 Alexandra Road,
Barnsley.

4th October 19—

Dear Miss Williams,

I would very much like to discuss with you the subject of Caroline's studies, mathematics in particular. I know she has never found this subject easy and that she is apt to be somewhat slow, though careful and conscientious, but now she is with Miss Brown for this subject she is finding things more difficult than ever. I am not implying any criticism of Miss Brown, whose teaching methods must of course be adapted to suit the class as a whole. My daughter feels, however, that she is often hurried on from one point to the next before she has fully grasped each one. I wonder if just a little more explanation from her teacher might not make all the difference. Caroline does try hard and very much wants to do well, so I feel she deserves sympathetic encouragement.

If you feel it would be useful, I could come and see you or Miss Brown and discuss the matter personally.

Yours sincerely,

Letter to a headmaster, complaining that a pupil is being bullied

9 Waverley Avenue,
London sw18 9ju.

J. Sinclair Esq., MA,
St George's School,
Southampton.   6th October 19—

Dear Mr Sinclair,

My son, James Fulton, a third-year boarder, has come home for the weekend in a very nervous state, and with bruises and cuts on his face. He will not tell me what has happened to him but I know he is not aggressive and I think he is being bullied by some of the older boys.

I would be very grateful if you could make inquiries and do all you can to make sure that a similar incident does not occur again.

Yours sincerely,

Letter asking that a pupil may be excused lessons

6 Alexandra Road,
Barnsley.

15th May 19—

Dear Miss Williams,

Would you kindly allow Caroline to leave school early on Thursday. I have to take her to the dentist and the only appointment I could make was for 3 o'clock. She would need to leave at about 2.30 to get to the surgery in time.

Yours sincerely,

Letter asking that a pupil may be excused games

9 Waverley Avenue,
London sw18 9JU.

J. Sinclair Esq., MA,
St George's School,
Southampton.

3rd March 19—

Dear Mr Sinclair,

   Would you please allow James to be excused all games lessons for the next two weeks. He has been ill during the holidays and is still rather weak.

Yours sincerely,

Letter to the principal of a school, giving notice that a pupil is to be taken away (1)

6 Alexander Road,
Barnsley.

5th December, 19—

Dear Miss Williams,

   My husband has just been offered a very good job in London and we will be moving to live there in a couple of months. I am therefore sorry to tell you that Caroline will be leaving the school at the end of the term. We are all very sorry that she will not be able to continue her studies with you but we have found an excellent school for her to attend in London and hope the move will not affect her studies unduly.

   May I take this opportunity to thank you for the kindness and attention you have always shown and for the excellent education my daughter has received with you.

Yours sincerely,

Letter to the principal of a school giving notice that a pupil is to be taken away (2)

9 Waverley Avenue,
London sw18 9ju.

J. Sinclair Esq., MA,
St George's School,
Southampton.

27th October 19—

Dear Mr Sinclair,

I am sorry to tell you that my wife and I have decided to take our son James away from St George's School at the end of next term and I am therefore giving you the required notice. We have been very concerned for some time about our son's behaviour and progress and we feel it might be best for him to attend a school nearer home where we can keep greater control over him.

Yours sincerely,

Letter of thanks to a son or daughter's tutor

311 Harts Way,
Somerford,
Cheshire.

4th September 19—

Dear Mr Evans,

I was delighted to learn that Patrick has passed his examinations and would like to thank you very much indeed for taking so much trouble with his coaching. Patrick tells me that you made even his least favourite subjects interesting and that he enjoyed working for you.

We are most grateful to you.

Yours sincerely,

Employment

Letter excusing absence from work

8 Shorts Walk,
Nuneaton,
Warwickshire.
Tel:

Mr W. James,
Holland Grey Ltd,
Nuneaton.   March 9th 19—

Dear Mr James,

I confirm that I telephoned you today to explain that I could not come into work as I was feeling ill. My doctor subsequently visited me and diagnosed influenza. As you will see from the enclosed medical certificate, I will probably be away from work for at least a week.

If there are any urgent problems about my work, please telephone me.

Yours sincerely,

Letter requesting leave of absence

8 Pearson Gardens,
Parkway,
South Yorkshire.

J. Simmons Esq.,
Simmons and Howard Ltd,
89 High Road,
Parkway,
South Yorks.   30th April 19—

Dear Mr Simmons,

I have just received a summons for jury service for two weeks
beginning 9th June. Could you therefore please give me
leave of absence for that period.

Yours sincerely,

Letter asking for promotion

23 Hazell Rise,
Carnforth,
Lancs.

H. Andrews Esq.,
Bairstow & Brooks Ltd,
West Street,
Carnforth.   7th January 19—

Dear Mr Andrews,

I understand that Mrs Green, the office manageress, is
leaving to have a baby and I would like to apply for her job.

As you know, I have been working here for over four
years as Mr Smith's secretary and feel I have gained a thorough
knowledge of the workings of the office. I also deputized for
Mrs Green for two weeks last year when she was on holiday.

Yours sincerely,

Application for an increase in salary

PRIVATE AND CONFIDENTIAL   Old Meadow Cottage,
                                  Littlebourne Road,
                                  Croydon,
                                  Surrey CR7 8JJ.

J. Marshall Esq.,
Hastings & Abbott Ltd,
7 Mace Street,
Croydon, Surrey CR7 9TP.   30th November 19—

Dear Mr Marshall,

   You may not be aware that although I have been
employed by the company for two years I have received
no increase in my salary of £X a year. During that time you
will appreciate that the cost of living has risen considerably and
I am finding it difficult to make ends meet. In addition, I
have been given greater responsibility since Mr Bass
retired.

   I would be grateful if you would give this matter your
consideration.

Yours sincerely,

Letter thanking employer for salary increase

Old Meadow Cottage,
Littlebourne Road,
Croydon,
Surrey CR7 8JJ.

J. Marshall Esq.,
Hastings & Abbott Ltd,
7 Mace Street,
Croydon, Surrey CR7 9TP.   5th December 19—

Dear Mr Marshall,

Thank you so much for increasing my salary by £X a year. You can be sure I will endeavour to justify the increase in every way.

Yours sincerely,

Letter of resignation from a post

10 Sheep Street,
Windsor,
Berks.

The Staff Manager,
Chase and Partridge Ltd,
8 Sutherland Avenue,
Windsor, Berks.   4th June 19—

Dear Sir,

I am writing to inform you that I have been offered a job as salesman with Brown and Maxwell of 75 Fordwych Road which I have accepted as the job offers me more responsibility and a larger salary.

In many ways I shall be sad to leave Chase and Partridge. I have certainly enjoyed the work and the friendship I have received from my colleagues. I am sure that the excellent training I have been given will stand me in good stead.

Yours faithfully,

Letter enquiring about possible job vacancies

7 Southampton Road,
Battersea,
London SW11 3FF.

Messrs. Spool and Paterson,
4 Church Walk,
London SW1 3PP.   6th March 19—

Dear Sirs,

I am writing to enquire whether you have any vacancies for an editorial assistant. I have always wanted to enter the publishing world and feel I would be well suited to this work. I have worked as a secretary in two publishing houses, often helping with proof-reading and picture research.

I am writing to your company because I have always been impressed with your books on sports and am particularly interested in this field as I participate in a number of sports.

I realize that I would have to start at the very bottom but I am anxious to learn and understand that this would be the best way to gain a thorough knowledge of publishing.

Yours faithfully,

Letter requesting a job application form

344 Stukeley Road,
Minehead,
Somerset.

The Personnel Manager,
Morcott, Lake and Co.,
Market Road,
Minehead,
Somerset   3rd June 19—

Dear Sir,

I have seen your advertisement in 'The Minehead News' for a Sales Manager and would be grateful if you would send me an application form for this post.

Yours faithfully,

Job application for a specific post

22 Barnes Road,
Leeds,
West Yorkshire.

Mason & Jones Ltd,
233–237 Honour Way,
Bradford.   7th July 19—

Dear Sirs,

I have seen your advertisement for a shorthand-typist in the 'Merrow Gazette' and wish to apply for the post.

I am 22 years old and was educated at St George's School where I obtained four GCE 'O' levels in English language, mathematics, history and biology. I also received two CSE passes in English literature and domestic science.

Since leaving school I have been employed by Merrow Travel Ltd as a junior shorthand-typist. My speeds are 120 wpm for shorthand and 60 wpm for typing. I am also experienced in audio-typing and book-keeping.

Although I have been given increasingly responsible work by my present employers, I would like to change my job to gain more experience.

I would be free for interview any evening after 5 p.m. My present employers have promised to give me a very favourable reference.

Yours faithfully,

Job application letter, enclosing curriculum vitae

88 Oakhill Close,
Portsmouth,
Hants.

Messrs Crease and Pendrigh, Solicitors,
7 Milton Way,
Portsmouth, Hants.   9th April 19—

Dear Sirs,

I read your advertisment for a litigation solicitor in the 'New Law Gazette' of 5th April and wish to apply for the position.

As you will see from the enclosed curriculum vitae, I have been employed by Sherwood District Council for the last two years. During that time I have gained extensive experience in all forms of litigation work including advocacy in magistrates', juvenile and county courts. Among other high court cases, I have been dealing with a complicated action for breach of contract which is expected to last three weeks.

My interests are rambling, golf, reading and amateur dramatics.

I would be available for interview at any time.

Yours faithfully,

Curriculum vitae to accompany a job application

Name: James Harper
Address: 22 Sidney Way, Sherwood
Telephone number—home: Sherwood 1234
office: Sherwood 5678

Date of birth: 24.8.19—
Marital status: single

Education since age 11: Oakleaf School, Wimbledon,
London sw19 8jh.
19— to 19—
6 'O' levels
3 'A' levels
English Grade B
French Grade A
History Grade C

Browning College, Oxbridge
19— to 19—
BA (law) Second Class Hons.

Further professional
qualifications: Law Society Final exams 19—
Employment: Articled clerk with Messrs Farnworth, Parker
and Co., The Dower House, Hope Street,
Melchester, 19— to 19—
(Admitted as solicitor 19—)
Assistant Solicitor, Sherwood District Council 19— to date
Persons from whom references may be obtained:
Mr S. Brand,
Sherwood District Council,
Town Hall,
Sherwood

Mr. G. N. Farnworth,
44 Downing Road,
Sherwood.

Letter accepting a post

                                              9 Ware Lodge,
                                              Ware Road,
                                              Bishops Stortford.

R. Beans Esq.,
Personnel Manager,
Multimec Ltd,
Hepple Rise,
Bishops Stortford.   27th July 19—

Dear Mr Beans,

   Thank you for your letter of 24th July offering me the post
of credit controller.

   I am delighted to accept this position and hope to start work
with you on 1st September. As you know I have to give my
present employers one month's notice.

Yours sincerely,

Letter to present employer applying for a reference

                                              9 Greenway Lane,
                                              Fowey,
                                              Cornwall.

Steven Bishop Esq.,
Limber Brothers Ltd,
Fowey, Cornwall.   23 June 19—

Dear Mr Bishop,

   I am applying for a post as printer at the Beehive Printing
Works, Bristol, and wonder if you would allow me to give
your name as a referee.

   Although I very much enjoy working for you, my wife and I

would like to return to Bristol to be near her mother who is rather elderly.

If my application is unsuccessful, I hope you will not feel I am dissatisfied with my job here. I am applying for this position for family reasons alone.

Yours sincerely,

Letter to previous employer applying for a reference

Bridge Cottage,
Simmons Lane,
Hurley,
Berks.

28th November 19—

Dear Mrs Berry,

I have just been offered the post of cook at the Malmswick Arms, Maidenhead and would be very grateful if you would give me a reference which I can send to my new employers. Will you please comment on my work and capabilities and my character. I think you were very satisfied with me during the four years I worked for you and I hope you will speak favourably of me.

Yours sincerely,

Letter giving a character reference

It is wise to send all references to a named person, wherever possible, marking the envelope 'Confidential'.

If you know of any serious reason why a person cannot be recommended for a job, you should say so. It is a good policy, however, not to give specific reasons, but rather to answer only the questions asked by the prospective employer. He will be able to draw his own conclusions from your reticence.

If you think highly of the person in question, you will of course point out all his or her good qualities, keeping these relevant to the nature of the job for which he or she is applying.

Welling School,
Welling Way,
Stoke-on-Trent.

Personnel Manager,
Forest, James and Drew Ltd,
34 Beak Road,
Stoke-on-Trent.   20th April 19—

Dear Sir,

In reply to your request for information about Susan Jones, who has applied for a post with your organization, she was a pupil at this school until eighteen months ago.

During the last year of her school career she was Head Girl and was extremely popular with both staff and pupils, who found her very fair. I could always trust her in every sphere of activity in which she had responsibility. She is an honest and straightforward person with a good sense of humour. I would unhesitatingly recommend her for the post for which she has applied.

If you require any further information please get in touch with me.

Yours faithfully,

Letter giving a favourable reference

Hambelside House,
Vicarage Rd,
Guildford, Surrey.

Dear Mrs Broadwood,

In reply to your letter, I am delighted to recommend Mrs Fielding as a daily help. She has been with me for three years and I have always found her hard-working, honest and cheerful.

Her reason for leaving me is that I am shortly moving from this area. I will be very sorry to lose her services.

Yours sincerely,

Letter giving a qualified reference

PRIVATE AND CONFIDENTIAL   119 Minster Road,
Weymouth,
Dorset.

Mrs M Briggs,
The Pines,
Oakham Way,
Weymouth.   30th May 19—

Dear Mrs Briggs,

Mrs J. O'Reilly, who worked for me as a housekeeper for two years, has asked me to give her a reference. Mrs O'Reilly is extremely capable and honest although in the last few months she worked for me she made a number of small mistakes and also took time off without adequate notice, putting a strain on the household. I feel she may have been in need of a change and in a new post you may find her work to be entirely satisfactory.

Yours sincerely,

Letter refusing a reference

CONFIDENTIAL

10 Eden Street,
Middlesbrough,
Cleveland.

The Personnel Manager,
G. Street & Co. Ltd,
11 High Road,
Cleveland.

7th March 19—

Dear Sir,

   In reply to your letter of 4th March, enquiring about
Miss Judy White, I regret that I am unable to recommend her
to you and told her so when she left us. In the circumstances
I prefer to say nothing further.

Yours faithfully,

Open reference

17 Maybury Lane,
Colchester,
Essex.

19 September 19—

To whom it may concern

   Mrs. J. Handswell has worked for me as a daily help and
cook for three years. A good cook, she is efficient in every way,
trustworthy and completely honest. She is leaving me
because she would like to work nearer the centre of town.
I shall be very sorry to part with her and wish her every
success in her future employment.

(signed) (Mrs) A. Howard

Letter agreeing to give a reference

Carrington House,
Leigh Way,
Stockport.

12th June 19—

Dear Mrs Sullivan,

Thank you for your letter asking me to give you a reference.
I have heard from Mrs Allnot and will be getting a letter
off to her as soon as I possibly can. I wish you every success
and hope you will obtain the post with her.

Yours sincerely,

Letter taking up a reference

Bradpole,
Bentley Lane,
Weybridge,
Surrey.

18th November 19—

Dear Mr Adams,

Mr Jack Harling of Upper Cottage, Back Lane, tells me
he was employed by you for six years as a handyman and
chauffeur. He has applied to me for a similar job and I would
be most grateful to you if you would let me know if you found
him capable, hard working and totally reliable, and also the
reason he left your employment. I am particularly anxious
to know if he is a safe driver and a reasonable mechanic.

It goes without saying that anything you say will be
treated with the strictest confidence.

I am enclosing a stamped addressed envelope for your reply.

Yours sincerely,

Request for temporary help

3 Hillside Drive,
Stoke Underton,
Somerset.

6th July 19—

Dear Mrs Langridge,

Mrs Barnes has given me your name and has told me you
have helped her on occasion. I wonder if you could come to
help me for a short period.

My husband's mother, who lives with us, is failing in health
and confined to her room. As we are hoping to take a
holiday next month, we need someone to take charge of the
house and look after her while we are away. The old lady is
quite independent as regards washing and dressing, etc.,
but needs someone to keep her room in order, make her bed,
shop and prepare the meals and generally look after things.
The ordinary work of the house is dealt with by our daily
help, who comes in each morning. We have quite a
pleasant house, with a garden and television, and are a
quarter of a mile from shops and buses.

If you are free to undertake this temporary position (we hope
to be away for the first three weeks in August) will you let
me know your terms. Then if it seems we can come to some
arrangement, perhaps you would come over one day for a
cup of tea, so that I can show you the house and introduce
you to my mother-in-law.

Yours sincerely,

Business correspondence

Letter changing a doctor (1)

9 Butlers Grove,
Sleaford, Lincs.

10th June 19—

Dear Dr Grove,

For some time I have felt rather unhappy about my wife
and myself being on your list. My wife's cough, for example,
has not improved as I feel it should. We realize how busy
your are and feel it would be better if we registered with
another doctor and tried a different course of treatment.

Yours sincerely,

Letter changing a doctor (2)

17 Brakes Way,
Richmond,
Surrey.

11th July 19—

Dear Dr Richardson,

As you know I have recently moved from central London
to Richmond and feel it would be wise to register with a
doctor in this area. Would you kindly accept this notification
of my withdrawal from your list. I am grateful to you for
all you have done for me over the years.

Yours sincerely,

Letter to a new doctor

9 Butlers Grove,
Sleaford, Lincs.

19th June 19—

Dear Dr Fredericks,

Further to my telephone conversation with your
receptionist, I am grateful that you are able to accept my wife
and myself as patients. We were formerly patients of
Dr Grove, but I have felt it wise for various reasons to
make a change.

Yours sincerely,

Letter to the Inland Revenue concerning a change in tax coding

9 Fawley Road,
Fleetwood,
Lancs.

21st June 19—

Reference:

Dear Sirs,

On 15th June I was married to Julia Susan Claypole,
formerly of 10 New Road, Battle. Would you therefore send
me any necessary forms to fill out so that you can make the
necessary alterations to my tax code.

Yours faithfully,

Letter engaging solicitor

1 Park Street,
Dorking,
Surrey.

8th October 19—

Dear Mr Crosby,

Your name has been given to me by Mr James Henderson for whom I understand you act in legal matters. I need the help of a solicitor experienced in house purchase, and would be grateful if you would act for me in this and other matters from now onwards. I look forward to hearing that you are able to do this.

Yours sincerely,

Letter changing solicitor

23 Station Road,
Birkenhead.
25th August 19—

Dear Sir,

As you know, I am the sole executor of the will drawn up by you for my late aunt, Mrs Sarah Daw. It would simplify matters considerably, and make things easier for me if this matter of my aunt's will were handled from now on by my own solicitors, Messrs Mann, Chandler and Nephew. Will you therefore please send them the relevant papers. If you will let me have your account for the work already done in the matter, I will attend to it at once.

Yours faithfully,

Letter to solicitor asking him to change will

58 Thorpe Mews,
Brighton Gate,
Debden.

L. O. T. Money Esq.,
Messrs Money & Money,
1 Border Bank Chambers,
High Street,
Debden, Essex.

5th May 19—

Dear Mr Money,

You will recall that I asked you to prepare a will for me two years ago which I subsequently executed.

I now wish to make a legacy of £X to my friend Mrs Margaret Collins of 50 Broadacre, Debden. I assume that it will be necessary for you to prepare a codicil to give effect to this.

I look forward to hearing from you as soon as possible.

Yours sincerely,

Letter instructing solicitor to prepare power of attorney

'Sea View',
North Street,
Hove, East Sussex.

G. Boot Esq.,
Messrs Doe and Row,
15 Market Street,
Worthington.

9th October 19—

Dear Mr Boot,

In four weeks' time I shall be going to France for six months and therefore wish to give my brother, Mr Alan Patrick Frost of 32 The Drive, Brampton, a general power of attorney so that he can act for me in my absence.

Would you please prepare the necessary document as soon as possible and send it to me for signature.

Yours sincerely,

Letter to a solicitor, asking him to pursue a debt

7 The Beeches,
Soner Road,
Hatfield.

Mr F. Herbert,
Messrs Terence and Matthews,
47 Barnslee Road,
Hatfield.

19th March 19—

Dear Mr Herbert,

I enclose copies of correspondence between myself and Mr Alan Thornton of 65 Woodlands Road, Barnet. You will note that a year ago I loaned him £X for a period of three months but that my attempts to recover the money after the three-month period was over have been unsuccessful.

Would you please write to Mr Thornton and tell him that although I regret having to threaten him with legal action I am concerned that he has taken advantage of a favour which I did for him when he was in difficult circumstances.

Yours sincerely,

Letter to solicitor, asking him to advise about a claim for damages against the writer

100 Jade Road,
Heathfield,
East Sussex.

W. Grundy Esq.,
Messrs Lewis and Grundy,
17 Castle Street,
Heathfield.   19th September 19—

Dear Mr Grundy,

I enclose a copy of a letter which a Mr Charles Goldwell has sent me from which you will note that he is claiming £X for the injuries he says he received and loss of earnings which he claims resulted from his being bitten by my dog on 15th July.

I cannot really see how my dog, which is a miniature poodle, could have injured Mr Goldwell so badly. Although my dog nipped him in the thigh I fail to see how this necessitated his staying away from work.

As the man is clearly trying to blow the whole incident out of proportion, I think that a solicitor's letter would be appropriate and should be grateful if you would write to him. Please let me know if you require any further information.

Yours sincerely,

Letter to solicitor, asking him about a claim for damages which the writer wishes to make

77 Tarrant Road,
Cambridge.

Mr J. Leyland,
Messrs Leyland and Butcher,
21 High View Road,
Cambridge.   24th February 19—

Dear Mr Leyland,

I should be grateful if you would advise me as to whether I can make a claim against the local council in connection with an injury which I suffered yesterday.

I was walking along Swinbourne Road near your offices when I tripped over a paving stone which was out of alignment with the rest of the pavement. On falling to the ground I cut my forehead so badly that I had to go to the hospital to have the wound treated and since I was also badly shocked by the incident I have been advised by the hospital to take a week off work.

I should be grateful if you would let me know what I can do. If you wish to discuss the matter further, I would be able to see you during my lunch hour after I return to work next week.

Yours sincerely,

Letter to a bank, opening a current account

High Trees,
Upper Lane,
Malmsbury,
Wilts.
Tel:

The Manager,
St Martin's Bank,
Kennet Street,
Malmsbury, Wilts.   10th June 19—

Dear Sir,

   I have just started work and would like to open an account
with your branch of the St Martin's Bank.

   I would be able to pay in £X immediately and my salary
of £X a month would be paid directly into my account by
credit transfer. My employers are Messrs Jameson and Brook
of 35 Bridge Street, Malmsbury. If you require a further
reference, Mr A. Poole of 17 Beech Square, Malmsbury, who
is a client of yours, will answer any questions you may have.

Yours faithfully,

Letter transferring money from one account to another

Mill House,
Leamington Spa Road,
Leamington Spa,
Warwicks.

Haymarket Bank,
21 Victoria Road,
Leamington Spa,
Warwicks.   1st September 19—

For the attention of the Manager

Dear Sir,

Would you please transfer £X from my current account
(Number 103) to my deposit account (Number 1907).

Yours faithfully,

Letter paying in a cheque

3 Shelley Road,
Lowestoft.

The Manager,
Midwest Bank,
59 High Street,
Lowestoft.   15th May 19—

Dear Sir,

I enclose Far East Bank cheque number 00723 for £X
drawn on the account of Mrs Karen Parker. I would be
grateful if you would credit it to my account, number 12074.

Yours faithfully,

Letter stopping payment of a cheque

Green Vista,
16 Glen Crescent,
Leeds.

The Manager,
Payne's Bank,
119 Bolway Street,
Leeds.   5th October 19—

Dear Sir,

Would you please stop payment of my cheque Number ——
for £X dated 28th September in favour of David Andrews
& Co.

I have checked with this firm and they have not received
my letter containing the cheque. I assume it has been lost
in the post.

Yours faithfully,

Letter instructing bank to pay standing order

9 Cherry Tree Drive,
Harlow, Essex.

The Manager,
Fines Bank,
23 Palmers Parade,
Harlow Old Town.   1st September 19—

Dear Sir,

I should be grateful if, until further notice, you would pay
£X on the first of each month, beginning 1st October 19—
into the account of The Sandworth Flower Arrangement and
Gardening Society, account number 58227, Jeeves Bank,

High Street, Dollis Hill, and debit my account with you, number 662834, accordingly.

Yours faithfully,

Letter instructing the bank to honour a signature

7 The Grove,
London NW4B 3NH.

The Manager,
National Chelsea Bank Ltd.,
150 Bridge Street,
London NW4A 6OJ.   4th September 19—

Dear Sir,

Miss L. Causton has resigned as Treasurer of the Greenleaf Drama Society and Mr J. F. McDonald has taken her place. Would you therefore please honour Mr McDonald's signature on cheques drawn on the Society's account (No. 12345). Cheques will still be countersigned by the Honorary Secretary Mr M. Elliott.

I enclose a specimen of Mr McDonald's signature.

Yours faithfully,

Letter about an overdraft

311 Crediton Lane,
Glasgow.

The Manager,
Barminster Bank Ltd.,
47 Hamble Street,
Glasgow.   18th June 19—

Dear Sir,

   I received your letter of 14th June this morning and was
horrified to learn that my account with you has been
overdrawn by £X.

   This has been rather a bad month for me since I have had
to settle a large number of bills. However I do hope you will
allow the overdraft to stand until the beginning of next
month, when I shall be paying in my usual salary cheque.

Yours faithfully,

Letter asking for overdraft facilities

G. J. Timms,
53 Maiden Lane,
Chepstow.

A. Williams Esq.,
Manager,
The Milestone Bank,
Parker Crescent,
Chepstow.   17th August 19—

Dear Mr Williams,

   I am setting up in business as a painter and decorator and
should be grateful if you would let me have overdraft
facilities up to £X. I may need this arrangement for about

eighteen months while I am building up my business.

Perhaps you would like me to call in to discuss this with you.

Yours sincerely,

Letter asking for advice about investments

7 Stonehouse Close,
Poole,
Dorset.

The Manager,
The South-West Bank,
Byfield Road,
Poole, Dorset.   9th January 19—

Dear Sir,

A relative has recently died leaving me £X in his will and I would like your advice as to how to invest this. Naturally I wish the investment to be as secure as possible. Have you any ideas?

Yours faithfully,

Letter instructing the bank to make investments

58 Calderwood Gardens,
Cirencester,
Gloucestershire.

The Manager,
The National Western Bank,
19 Stratton Avenue,
Cirencester.   18th May 19—

Dear Sir,

Following our meeting last week, I have studied the list of
suggestions which you prepared for me and should be
grateful if you would invest £X for me in 9½% Environment
stock and £X in Batkin Ltd at Xp per share.

It will be convenient for me to call at the Bank in my
lunch-hour to sign any necessary documents.

Yours faithfully,

Letter asking a bank to make enquiries

8 Phoenix Walk,
Edmonton,
London N18 5SD.

W. K. Steeples Esq.,
The Manager,
The National Western Bank,
91 New Hill Road,
Edmonton, N18 6JY.   26th June 19—

Dear Mr Steeples,

I am considering letting a room in my house to
Mr Simon Makepeace of 11 Acacia Grove, Edmonton, who

has given The Midwest Bank, 71 Barley Road, Edmonton as a referee.

Would you please make the necessary enquiries and let me know whether in the bank's opinion, he would be able to afford a rent of £X a month.

Yours sincerely,

Letter asking for increase in credit limit on a credit card

18 Bishops Drive,
Hull.

Borrowcard Ltd.,
Long Lane,
London WIB 7HF

27th February 19—

Dear Sirs,

Borrowcard Number 56789

I would be most grateful if you would increase my credit limit on the above credit card to £X per month. I do a great deal of business entertaining and use my card to pay restaurant bills.

Yours faithfully,

Letter enclosing a cheque in settlement of an account

'Minnings',
9 Lavender Hill,
Sileby,
Leics.

J. Morris and Co.,
925 Grove Road,
Sileby.

28th April 19—

Dear Sirs,

I enclose my cheque for £X in full settlement of your account, number 09087 dated 14th April. Would you please let me have your receipt.

Yours faithfully,

Letter enclosing a cheque in part settlement of an account

29 Montrose Terrace,
Twynholm,
Kirkcudbrightshire.

Makewells Ltd,
7 Winston Crescent,
Tamworth, Staffs.

29th May 19—

Dear Sirs,

I enclose my cheque for £X in part settlement of your account number 58749 dated 4th April 19—. I will let you have a cheque for the balance in a fortnight's time and hope the delay will not inconvenience you. Will you please acknowledge receipt of this letter.

Yours faithfully,

Letter to store, opening an account

19 Westview Drive,
Margate,
Kent.

Messrs Graham and Pultney,
Pine Road,
Margate.

30th June 19—

Dear Sirs,

As I shop in your store extremely frequently it would be **very** useful for me to have a credit account with you. Please let me know whether this can be arranged.

Yours faithfully,

Letter to hotel, enquiring about facilities for a private function

9 Bevis Mansions,
Connaught Street,
Hull.

Private Functions Department,
Queensway Hotel,
Carne Road,
Hull, Humberside.

5th January 19—

Dear Sirs,

We are planning a buffet lunch party for our daughter's birthday on 19th February and the Queensway Hotel has been recommended to us. We expect to invite about fifty guests and would be grateful if you could send us specimen menus, wine lists and details of your room hire charges. Would you also confirm that the Tower Suite is free on the date we have chosen.

Yours faithfully,

Letter to caterer or hotel, booking a private function

9 Bevis Mansions,
Connaught Street,
Hull.

Private Functions Department,
Queensway Hotel,
Carne Road,
Hull, Humberside.

9th January 19—

Dear Sirs,

Thank you for your letter of 8th January, confirming that the Tower Suite is available for hire on 19th February and enclosing specimen finger and fork buffet menus.

I confirm my booking of the Tower Suite from 12 midday till 4 p.m. on 19th February for about fifty guests. I have chosen fork buffet menu 5 and would like your carafe white wine to be served. Could you please let me know how much wine you suggest for each person.

Perhaps I could call in and discuss details with you one afternoon next week.

Yours faithfully,

Letter to a building society, withdrawing money

9 Forest Approach,
Warwick.

The Manager,
Moors Building Society,
West Bromwich.   25th March 19—

Dear Sir,

I would like to withdraw £X from my account
(number 1997) with your Society and am writing to give you
one month's notice, as required by Rule 15 of the Society. I
enclose my pass book.

Yours faithfully,

Letter to insurance company, insuring an article

11 Forest Drive,
Durham.

General and Royal Insurance Ltd,
118 Wilberforce Road,
London W1J 2HG.   14 July 19—

Dear Sirs,

Further to my telephone conversation, I would like to take
out, with immediate effect, an 'all-risks' insurance policy on my
diamond ring. I enclose a copy of the jeweller's valuation
from which you will see that the ring is worth £X.

Please send me a cover note and let me know what
premium is payable.

Yours faithfully,

Letter to insurance company regarding car insurance

26 Hazell Way,
Worcester Park,
Surrey.

Beefeater Insurance Co. Ltd,
Threadneedle Street,
London.

4th December 19—

Dear Sirs,

I am considering buying a —— car and before making a
final decision, I should be grateful if you would let me have
full details of your motor insurance policies. Would you please
let me know the terms for Comprehensive and for Third
Party Insurance.

I am intending to use the car for journeys of about X miles
(kilometres) a week in connection with my employment.
Would you please let me know what extra premium would be
payable. I would also like to know the difference in cost
between allowing any driver to use the car, with my consent,
and restricting the drivers to my wife and myself.

I have been driving regularly for about three years, without
accident, although I have never owned a car before. My
wife has only recently passed her driving test.

I look forward to hearing from you.

Yours faithfully,

Letter reporting a car accident and making an insurance claim

Magpie Cottage,
Woodbury Hill,
Woodstock,
Oxon.

Beefeater Insurance Co. Ltd,
Threadneedle Street,
London.

28th May 19—

Policy Number JH 10945

Dear Sirs,

I have to report that this morning, whilst driving out of Henderson Drive, I scraped the side of a car travelling along the main Oxford Road. Both cars are badly scratched and my off-side bumper is dented. In the event of the repairs costing £X or more, I wish to give notice that I shall claim under my policy with you.

The driver of the other car (registration number XXXXX) is Mr Mark French of 9 Fenwick Street, Oxford. He is insured with the President Insurance Company.

Yours faithfully,

Your home

Letter to an estate agent, asking for details of properties for sale

67 Grafton Road,
Loughton, Essex.

Messrs Drew and Batchelor,
Estate Agents,
90 Upper Mall,
Loughton.

5th April 19—

Dear Sirs,

I am looking for a three-bedroomed house, if possible with a garage, in a quiet street in this area. I am able to pay up to £X. Could you please let me have details of houses which might be suitable.

Yours faithfully,

Letter to a private advertiser about a house for sale

67 Grafton Road,
Loughton, Essex.

Dear Sir,

I have seen your advertisement in the local newspaper for a two-bedroomed, semi-detached house. Will you please let me have further details.

Yours faithfully,

Letter to estate agent making an offer for a property

67 Grafton Road,
Loughton, Essex.

Messrs Drew and Batchelor,
Estate Agents,
90 Upper Mall,
Loughton.

23rd August 19—

Dear Sirs,

15 Pear Tree Close

    Would you please find out if the owner will sell this
property for £X, subject to contract. This price would
include the fitted carpets and curtains. I think the asking price
is somewhat high, especially as the house needs painting
outside.

Yours faithfully,

Letter to owner of house or flat for sale, making an offer

*It is essential to include the wording 'subject to contract' when
making an offer for the purchase of a property to avoid entering
into a binding contract before actual exchange of contracts.*

103 Peverell Road,
Wigan,
Greater Manchester.
8th March 19—

Dear Mr Frank,

    Thank you for showing us the house again on Saturday. My
wife and I like it very much and wonder if you would

consider an offer of £X for it, subject to contract. This price would include all curtains and fitted carpets.

If you agree to sell the house to me would you please send me the name and address of your solicitor so that I can ask my solicitor to write to him.

Yours sincerely,

Letter to a solicitor about house or flat purchase

89 Thornton Way,
Warrington, Cheshire.
22nd August 19—

Dear Mr Greaves,

Further to our telephone conversation, would you please offer £X for 4 Lulworth Court, Berwick Street, Warrington. The owner is Mr James Marks. I answered his advertisement in the local newspaper, so there is no estate agent involved. I do not know who his solicitors are.

Assuming he accepts my offer, perhaps you would let me know when I should pay a deposit.

Yours sincerely,

Letter to assurance brokers, or assurance company, regarding combined life assurance and house purchase

7 Tolladine Road,
Woodford,
Essex.

Brown & Jones (Insurance Brokers) Ltd,
63 Farborough Road,
Woodford,
Essex.   19th March 19—

Dear Sirs,

I am looking for a house in the Chelmsford area and would like some preliminary information about endowment mortgages. I am particularly interested in a 'with profits' policy.

I was 29 years old on my last birthday and am in good health. I would of course be willing to undergo a medical examination should this be required. I would like to spread the payments over 25 years. My salary is £X per annum and I have £X capital.

Yours faithfully,

Letter to building society, enquiring about mortgage facilities

7 King's Court,
Medway Road,
Sandy,
Bedfordshire.

The Manager,
Newtown Building Society,
Shaftesbury Drive,
Luton, Bedfordshire.   12th October 19—

Dear Sir,

My wife and I would like to buy a house in the Luton area and we wish to enquire what the position would be regarding a mortgage.

We are both working full time, my wife as a secretary, currently earning £X per annum and myself as a computer programmer with a salary of £X per annum. We have had some £X deposited at your branch for eighteen months.

Perhaps you would let me know whether you would be prepared to consider our application and give us some indication of the amount you might be prepared to lend us.

Yours faithfully,

Letter applying for a mortgage

7 King's Court,
Medway Road,
Sandy, Beds.

The Manager,
Newtown Building Society,
Shaftesbury Drive,
Luton, Beds.

6th November 19—

Dear Sir,

You will recall that I wrote to you on 12th October asking whether you would grant my wife and me a mortgage. At that time you replied saying you might lend us up to £X.

We have now found a freehold house at 17 Smith Street, Sandy, and our offer of £X has been accepted by the vendor. The house, which is approximately 20 years old, has two reception rooms, three bedrooms, a garage and a small garden.

We would be able to raise £X but require a mortgage of £X. I would be grateful if you would consider this matter quickly as the vendor wishes to exchange contracts as soon as possible.

Yours faithfully,

Letter to building society, asking for terms to pay off a mortgage

8 Lorne Gardens,
Marden, Kent.

The Manager,
Harley Building Society,
17 High Road,
Margate, Kent.

22nd February 19—

Dear Sir,

I am considering paying off the mortgage on my house by a lump sum and would be grateful if you would let me know if the Society would agree to this and if so, what sum would be payable to the Society. I believe you would charge a commission on the balance outstanding and I would like details of this.

Yours faithfully,

Letter to landlord, asking for time to pay rent

57 Paragon Drive,
Blackburn.

I. Gould Esq.,
33 Bewdley Crescent,
Blackburn.

12th May 19—

Dear Mr Gould,

As you may know, I have recently had a bad accident which meant that I was absent from work for two months. Consequently my finances are in a state of complete disarray, while my commitments have been even more pressing.

I should therefore be most grateful if you would allow me to delay paying this month's rent until the beginning of next month when I anticipate that my routine will be back to normal. Naturally I will let you have two months' rent at that time.

Yours sincerely,

Letter to landlord asking for repairs to be done

3 The Parade,
Tywyn,
Gwynedd.

Mr D. Pepper,
58 Napoleon Drive,
Eastley.   14th October 19—

Dear Mr Pepper,

During the last week my bedroom ceiling has developed a large crack running across the entire length of the room and small pieces of plaster have been falling from the ceiling. I should therefore be grateful if you would arrange for your builder to inspect the property before the situation gets any worse.

Yours sincerely,

Letter to landlord, asking him to cancel a lease

28 The Vale,
Fulham,
sw6 8nm.

7th March 19—

Dear Sir,

The executors have now wound up the estate of my late
husband and it is necessary for me to reduce my expenses
drastically if I am to live within the income remaining to me.
I must therefore, with great regret, seek a smaller house,
and my object in writing is to ask if you will terminate the
agreement you made with us.

I realize I have power to sub-let the premises, but am
reluctant to incur the responsibility which this would entail,
and should therefore be so very grateful if you would allow me
to vacate the house on 31st May instead of holding me to the
strict letter of the agreement.

Yours faithfully,

Letter to landlord, asking for permission to sub-let

7 French Street,
London nw5r 8qw.

8th November 19—

Dear Mr Jacobs,

Now my son has left home this house is rather large for me
and I would very much like to sub-let the top floor. Through a
mutual friend, I have found an extremely suitable tenant,
Miss Elizabeth Belling of 19 Weymont Street, Kilburn,
whose references are entirely satisfactory.

Under my agreement with you I need your written permission to sub-let and I very much hope you will be able to grant my request. I would be glad to have an answer as soon as possible, so that I can let Miss Belling know your decision.

Yours sincerely,

Letter to a builder asking for an estimate

73 Charlotte Street,
Bolton,
Lancs.

J. Ramshackle and Son Ltd,
Builders,
37 Cypress Parade,
Bolton, Lancs.   23rd August 19—

Dear Sirs,

I would like a storm porch built at the front of my house and should be grateful if you would send along one of your people to give me an estimate.

I would like the work to be completed before October. Would you please let me know whether this would be possible?

Yours faithfully,

Letters of complaint

Think twice before writing a letter of complaint. It is always best to deal with a complaint verbally if you can, to avoid the possibility that your letter will be misunderstood. If the occasion arises when a complaint needs to be put in writing, think yet again. Do not write anything until you have considered the matter calmly.

If you have written a letter of complaint and do not get the results you want from it you may find it useful to contact your local council (trading standards department, or environmental health department), consumer advice centres if they operate in your area, Citizens' Advice Bureaux, or the Office of Fair Trading. Most firms or public bodies belong to a professional or trade association to whom you can also write. Trade associations often provide a conciliation service and will investigate individual complaints and give advice. Try writing to the local newspaper as well.

If all else fails, take the matter to your solicitor or perhaps to a neighbourhood law centre if there is one in your district.

Letter of complaint to dry cleaners

94 Mitre Lane,
Epping, Essex.

The Manager,
Kleenissimo Cleaners,
5 Duke Street,
Epping,
Essex.   12th December 19—

Dear Sir,

I left a cashmere coat at your shop to be dry-cleaned on 4th December and collected it yesterday. Before putting it on at home I noticed a large hole in the back of the garment which was not there before I brought the coat to you.

When I came in to see you today your assistant told me that your firm accepted no liability for any damage whatsoever caused to articles of clothing in the course of dry-cleaning.

This is to inform you that unless you let me have £X, representing the cost of a new coat of the same type, I shall put the matter in the hands of my solicitor.

Yours faithfully,

Letter complaining about delay in delivering goods

7 Barwell Way,
Warwick.

Groots Bulbfields Ltd,
Spalding,
Lincs.   17th September 19—

Dear Sirs,

On 8th August I ordered a quantity of bulbs from you and you promised to deliver them within ten days. It is now 17th September and despite two telephone calls to your offices I have still not received the bulbs.

If you are unable to send me the bulbs immediately please cancel my order. The bulbs will be of no use to me after 25th September and I will have to refuse to accept them after that date.

Yours faithfully,

Letter to merchant about unsolicited goods

A private person who receives unsolicited goods and does not want them must allow the sender to take the goods back within six months after he has received them. After the six month period, provided he has not agreed to return them, the goods become his property and he can do what he wishes with them.

Within the six-month period however, the recipient can give written notice to the sender of the goods, giving his name and address and stating that the goods are unsolicited. The sender then has thirty days to collect them and if he fails to do so they become the recipient's property at the end of the thirty days. The recipient does not therefore have to wait until the six month period has expired.

If the sender demands payment for the goods, or threatens proceedings, he can be prosecuted.

> 70 Marsh Lane,
> Canonbury,
> London NIR 4WW.

The Sales Manager,
Hemmings and Fife Ltd,
74 Brick Street,
London W14A 5RE.   30th June 19—

Dear Sir,

This morning I received a parcel of woollen material from your warehouse. I did not order this material and would ask you to arrange for your parcel to be collected within the next 30 days. If it is not collected within this time I shall sell the material.

Kindly note that I do not wish to receive any more goods from you.

Yours faithfully,

124

Letter disputing an account

9 Glebe Road,
Colwyn Bay,
N. Wales.

Accounts Department,
S. Fitzgerald Ltd,
Colwyn Bay,
N. Wales.

15th February 19—

Dear Sirs,

I have received your invoice for £X and notice that you
have charged me for five pairs of sheets whereas I only ordered
and received three pairs.

I enclose my cheque for £X which covers the cost of the
three pairs of sheets. Would you please let me have
your receipt.

Yours faithfully,

Letter of complaint to a neighbour

88 Rocks Lane,
Sidcup,
Kent.

3rd January 19—

Dear Mr Mills,

I have already spoken to you several times about your
dog coming into my garden and digging up my lawn. I must
ask you to try to control him, otherwise I will be forced to go to
my solicitor about the problem. Of course I very much hope
this will not be necessary.

Yours sincerely,

Reply to above

86 Rocks Lane,
Sidcup,
Kent.

Dear Mr Barnes,

I was most distressed to learn that my dog has managed
to get into your garden again and that he has been causing
damage. I have asked my children to make sure the gate is
securely shut but I think it has been left open and the dog has
got out. I am extremely sorry for the inconvenience and
would like to pay for the damage to the lawn.

Yours sincerely,

Letter to the local council

12 Maidstone Crescent,
Fenshurst,
Cleveland.

The Borough Engineer,
Fenshurst Borough Council,
Municipal Offices,
High Road,
Fenshurst,
Cleveland.   7 March 19—

Dear Sir,

I am writing to complain about the appalling state of the
roadway in Maidstone Crescent. There are pot-holes in
several places along the road and there is scarcely an area of
road surface which is even. Consequently driving a car along it
is a hazardous business.

I have lived in Maidstone Crescent for five years and

during that time no repairs have been carried out to the road surface. Would you therefore please ensure that something is done as soon as possible, before there is a serious accident.

Yours faithfully,

Letter to local councillor

15 Acacia Avenue,
Brandreth,
Humberside.

Councillor Leonard Reason, JP,
23 Kingston Way,
Brandreth,
Humberside.   5th June 19—

Dear Councillor Reason,

As a member of the Council's Planning Committee and Council Member for this ward, you will be aware that the Committee, at its meeting next Wednesday, will be discussing an application for planning permission for the construction of a block of private flats on the site of numbers 12 and 14 Acacia Avenue, which is opposite my home.

You were also present at the meeting last Thursday of the Acacia Avenue Residents' Association when all the residents who were there expressed their hostility to the scheme.

I therefore hope that you will represent our interests at the Planning Committee meeting and try to ensure that planning permission is refused.

Yours sincerely,

Letter to Member of Parliament

27 Marion Way,
Norcastle,
Derbyshire.

George Cousins Esq., QC, MP,
House of Commons, SW1.

18th January 19—

Dear Mr Cousins,

I feel I should write to you about a serious injustice which my son Tony has recently suffered.

Two months ago he applied for a job as Assistant Personnel Manager at Sampsons Seed Drills, the largest employers in Norcastle. Tony has had an excellent record in personnel management and hoped at least to be given an interview.

Unfortunately two years ago Tony was off work for three months suffering from severe depression and had to attend St Mark's Hospital Psychiatric Department as an out-patient. His illness was, however, only temporary and since going back to work his health and progress have been excellent; at no other time in his life has he suffered from any other serious illness, mental or otherwise.

Tony received a letter from Sampsons which referred to the period of depression Tony mentioned in his application form and said that because of this the company could not consider him in any capacity. Tony and I were very upset by this letter, not the least because it seems to imply that because of one short period of depression Tony may be branded, at least by Sampsons, as a mentally ill person for the rest of his life.

Would you please do what you can to remedy this injustice and at the least try to bring home to Sampsons the potentially damaging effect of their decision.

Yours sincerely,

Travel and holidays

Letter confirming travel arrangements

12 Beehive Lane,
Epsom, Surrey.

The Manager,
Sunway Travel Agency,
7 High Street,
Esher, Surrey.

1st December 19—

Dear Sir,

Further to our telephone conversation this morning,
I confirm that you are reserving two seats for me on
flight BA 123 for Paris leaving Heathrow at 2 p.m.
on 15th December. I enclose my cheque for £X in payment.

Please send me any flight information with the tickets.

Thank you for your help.

Yours faithfully,

Letter enquiring about hotel accommodation

110 Westfield Road,
Mansfield,
Nottinghamshire.

Mrs B. Evans,
White Cliffs Guest House,
Folkestone, Kent.

10th April 19—

Dear Mrs Evans,

Your guest house has been recommended to me by a
friend, Mrs Mary Simmons. Would you please send me

details of your terms and let me know if you have any vacancies during July.

We would need two double rooms, facing the sea; one room would be for my husband and myself and the other for our two sons aged 5 and 8. We also have a small baby who could sleep in our room. Could you provide a cot for him? We would also ideally like to hire a high-chair.

Would you please let me know if there is any reduction for children. Would you have any objections to a small, quiet and well-trained dog? We would like to spend a fortnight or three weeks at Folkestone.

Yours sincerely,

Letter concerning lost property

7 Peaven Close,
Hertford.

The Manager,
White House Hotel,
Perling Road, Whitby.

19th August 19—

Dear Sir,

I confirm my telephone call of this morning when I informed you that on my return home today from a stay at your hotel I found my pearl ear-rings were missing. I imagine I left them on the dressing table in room 5, or possibly in the bathroom.

The ear-rings are quite valuable and also have sentimental associations. If you find them I would very much appreciate your telephoning me and if you could return them by registered mail, I would gladly refund the postage.

Yours faithfully,

Your club or society, charity work

Letter applying for membership of a club

19 Belmont Drive,
Slough, Bucks.

The Hon. Secretary,
Meadowlands Lawn Tennis and Squash Club,
Bainthorne Drive,
Slough.   13th May 19—

Dear Sir,

I have recently moved to this area and would very much
like to become a member of your club.

I am a very experienced tennis player, though I have only
recently taken up the game of squash.

Could you please let me know if you have any vacancies. I
regret that, being new to the district, I do not know anyone
to introduce me to the club.

Yours faithfully,

Letter to secretary of club proposing a friend as a member

15 Newport Green Drive,
Basingstoke,
Hants,
RG22 6LM.
Tel:

S. Brand Esq.,
Secretary,
Daybrook Road Squash Club,
Daybrook Road,
Basingstoke,
Hants.   23rd October 19—

Dear Mr Brand,

I shall be grateful if you would put up the name of
Mr Alex McDougall of 18 Railton Road, Basingstoke for
election at the next Committee meeting on Tuesday
7th November. I shall be proposing him, seconded by
Mr Laurence Bryant.

When I was a student at Reading I played regularly with
Mr McDougall, who was then living in the area. I found him
to be an exhilarating opponent and therefore feel that he would
be an asset to the club.

Yours sincerely,

Letter accepting club membership application

West Avenue Bridge Club,
17 West Avenue,
London N21.

19th August 19—

Dear Mr Whitney,

Thank you for your letter of 12th August. We have been unable to accept new members for the past year as we had reached our limits of membership. However you may be lucky now because two vacancies have been created by the resignation of two members. Since you are new to the area, why not come down to the club next Wednesday evening at 7.30 and meet some of my colleagues on the committee? Subject to your still wishing to be a member I will propose you for election at the committee meeting on the following Thursday.

Yours sincerely,

Letter from the club secretary, informing applicant of his election

Green Fields Cricket Club,
9 Harvester Road,
Penge SE20.

John Bishop Esq.,
Willow Cottage,
Madell Way,
Penge SE20.   12th June 19—

Dear Mr Bishop,

I am pleased to inform you that you were elected a member of the Green Fields Cricket Club at the Committee meeting on

Thursday 10th June. I enclose the club's fixture card and a copy of the rules.

I shall be grateful if you would let me have a cheque for £X to cover your entrance fee and first year's subscription.

Yours sincerely,

Letter from club secretary informing applicant that he has not been elected

Boston Hill Tennis Club,
8 Boston Lane,
Bradford.

Miss Leonie Platt,
77 Barn Road,
Bradford.   11th May 19—

Dear Miss Platt,

I regret to inform you that at the meeting of the Boston Hill Tennis Club on Thursday 8th May your name was put forward for election but that you were unsuccessful.

I should however point out that there were nine applicants for four vacancies and that should you wish your name to be submitted to the committee in a few months' time you may be more successful.

Yours sincerely,
Hon. Secretary.

Letter from club secretary, asking for payment of subscription

> Old Marronians C.C.,
> Weston Green,
> Ipswich IP2 3JR.

Peter Stuart Esq.,
78 River Road,
Ipswich IP5 7PQ.   5th May 19—

Dear Mr Stuart,

Your subscription of £X, due on the first of last month, has not yet reached us. I expect the matter has escaped your attention and look forward to receiving your cheque as soon as possible.

Yours sincerely,
Hon. Secretary.

A repeated request for an unpaid subscription

> Old Marronians C.C.,
> Weston Green,
> Ipswich IP2 3JR.

Peter Stuart Esq.,
78 River Road,
Ipswich IP5 7PQ   25th May 19—

Dear Mr Stuart,

I wrote to you on 5th May, reminding you that your annual subscription, due on 1st April, had not been paid.

Your cheque has still not reached me and I must draw your attention to the Club rules. Rule XX states that any member

135

whose subscription remains unpaid for two months, ceases
to be a member and can be refused re-election.

The Committee would be very distressed to have to
enforce this rule in your case, especially as you are a founder
member of the Old Marronians. Please let us have your
cheque by return, so we shall not be forced to ask you to
leave the club.

Yours sincerely,
Hon. Secretary.

Letter from a club secretary, asking a member to resign

> Bicks Hill Horticultural Society,
> Lower Bicks Hill,
> Derby.

R. Davidson Esq.,
6 Summer Street,
Derby.   7th August 19—

Dear Mr Davidson,

As you know, our Committtee has now looked into the
circumstances surrounding the incident at the Rose Show at
the end of last month. I regret that we have decided that we
must ask for your resignation, in the interests of all the
members of this Society.

Please let me have your letter of resignation within the next
week, so that this matter can be resolved speedily and without
embarrassment on either side.

Yours sincerely,
Hon. Secretary.

Letter of resignation from a club

8 Osborne Road,
Ellesmere, Salop.

The Hon. Secretary,
The Brooks Cricket Club,
Ellesmere, Salop.   9th June 19—

Dear Sir,

I regret that I must tender my resignation as a member
of the Brooks Cricket Club. I am very sorry to have to do this
but my doctor has advised me not to play any longer.

Yours faithfully,

Letter inviting a celebrity to give a talk

Black Fen Horticultural Society,
Upper Woolbridge Street,
Warminster, Wilts.

Jack Tumbleweed Esq.,
The Hall,
Wayley, Wiltshire.   17th April 19—

Dear Mr Tumbleweed,

I realize that as a famous television gardening personality
your time is very limited, but I would be very grateful
indeed if you could spare an evening to come and talk at
one of the weekly meetings of our society.

The Black Fen Horticultural Society is a very
long-established organization with about 500 keen members
who attend our meetings regularly, bringing their

families and friends. We also run many competitions throughout the year.

We have not yet finalized our programme for this season and would be more than happy to welcome you as a guest speaker on any Thursday evening, from 7.30 p.m. at our meetings in the Memorial Hall, Upper Woolbridge Street.

We would not be able to pay you a fee but of course we will settle your travelling expenses and can also arrange over-night accommodation.

Perhaps you could let me know which dates would be most suitable for you. We all very much hope you will be able to come and talk to us and look forward to hearing from you in the near future.

Yours sincerely,

Thanks afterwards

Black Fen Horticultural Society,
Upper Woolbridge Street,
Warminster, Wilts.

Jack Tumbleweed Esq.,
The Hall,
Wayley, Wiltshire.   3rd June 19—

Dear Mr Tumbleweed,

Thank you so much for coming to talk to the Black Fen
Horticultural Society last Thursday. It was one of the most
interesting and lively evenings we have ever had and I am sure
we shall all benefit from your practical advice on growing
roses.

It was a great pleasure for us all to meet you and also to
meet your wife. We hope you will pay us a return visit in
the not-too-distant future. You will always be most welcome.

Thank you once again.

Yours sincerely,

Letter requesting someone to serve on a committee

6 The Grove,
Little Rustington,
Dorset.
18th July 19—

Dear Mrs Thomas,

I know how many calls you have upon your time, but I am wondering if you would feel able to undertake one more activity in a very worthy cause.

As you perhaps know, Jane Smith is leaving the district, and this leaves a vacancy upon the committee of our local branch of the Children's Aid Society, which Jane helped to start.

It has been suggested that you might be willing to serve upon this committee – we do need somebody active and with lots of good ideas, to take her place! Should you feel able to undertake this, it would entail a monthly committee meeting and some work in connection with our annual fête.

If you are willing to be co-opted to the committee I will bring forward your name at the next meeting.

Yours sincerely,

Reply to above

Highfield Cottage,
Great Rustington,
Dorset.

21 July 19—

Dear Mrs Feverel,

Thank you for your letter about the C.A.S. Jane Smith will
be greatly missed and it will be no easy task for anyone to
take her place, but if you think I can help I shall be most
happy to serve in any way I can. No doubt you will be
letting me know if the matter is confirmed by the committee.

Yours sincerely,

Letter requesting a titled lady to open a Fête

6 The Grove,
Little Rustington,
Dorset.
20th April 19—

Dear Lady Cummings,

The Little Rustington branch of the Children's Aid Society
is planning to hold a small garden fête in May and the
Committee would feel honoured if you would agree to
perform the opening ceremony.

No doubt you already know of this worthy cause which for
some years now has brought help and comfort in varied ways,
to those who are suffering through no fault of their own.
I enclose one of the most recent leaflets about the work. We
want to make our fête a really successful effort and the
presence of yourself as patron would undoubtedly be a very
great help to the cause.

We have not finally settled upon the actual date, as

knowing how busy your ladyship is, we felt it might be preferable for you to name the most convenient day. The Vicar has kindly agreed to lend us the Vicarage garden on any Saturday in the second half of May.

May we hope that you will help our cause in this way?

Yours truly,
Hon. Sec.

Letter requesting a celebrity to present prizes

209 Huniton Road,
West Hampstead,
London NW6 3JS
14th April 19—

Dear Mr Baxter,

On 4th August we will be holding a charity cricket match to raise funds for the local boys' club. On behalf of the organizing committee I am writing to ask you to honour us with your presence and present the cup to the winning team.

I know you are an extremely busy man but if you are free on the afternoon of 4th August we would be so grateful if you could give us your support. We are certain that if you agree to help us the success of the day will be assured.

Perhaps you would let me know as soon as possible if you can come and how much your fee would be.

Yours sincerely,

Letter requesting a donation

174 Washpool Road,
Barnet.

Maxwell James Publishers Ltd,
235 High Road,
Barnet.   20th June 19—

Dear Sirs,

On 19th July we are holding a book sale at the parish hall to raise funds for the repairs to the church roof. At least £X is needed to save the roof of this historic church, which dates from the fifteenth century.

We are wondering if you might be able to spare some slightly damaged or out-of-print books or alternatively if you might make a donation to our funds. We could of course arrange to collect any books you might be able to spare.

Yours faithfully,

Letter requesting patronage of a fund-raising effort

The Warren,
Rustington Peverel,
Berkshire.

23rd April 19—

My Lord (or, Dear Sir),

On behalf of the Rustington Peverel Community Association, may I request your (Lordship's) patronage of our forthcoming Fête and Sale of Work on June 11th. It is to be held in an effort to raise funds for the building of a new wing for the Social Centre in the village. This institution, which has been established several years, is greatly in need of increased accommodation, owing to the large number of new residents in the satellite town being developed adjoining the village. I enclose a copy of the last Annual Report, which describes in detail the very excellent work of the Social Centre.

The Committee is most anxious to make a real success of the fête on June 11th, and if your Lordship will allow us to include your name as a Patron, the Committee will feel much honoured and greatly indebted.

I have the honour to be
Your Lordship's obedient servant,
(or, Yours faithfully,)

Letter thanking a patron (1)

6 The Grove,
Little Rustington,
Dorset.
30 May 19—

Dear Lady Cummings,

The Committee have asked me to express to you their
very sincere thanks for your gracious help in opening the fête
last Saturday. Your help in this way not only contributed
greatly towards the very successful financial result (the final
sum collected is £X) but much enhanced the pleasure of the
occasion for everyone. Thank you so much.

Yours sincerely,
Hon. Sec.

Letter thanking a patron (2)

The Warren,
Rustington Peverel
Berkshire.
11th May 19—

My Lord,

The Committee acknowledge the receipt of your Lordship's
letter of the 9th May, would like to express their gratitude
for the cheque which accompanied it and for your kindness
in consenting to patronize our Fête and Sale of Work.

The Committee wish me to say how deeply they value
your Lordship's interest and generosity and to express their
sincere thanks for your valuable co-operation in our work.

I have the honour to be
Your Lordship's most obedient servant,

Requests with replies

Letter asking a friend for a letter of introduction (1)

> 19 Cranleigh Gardens,
> Brighton.
>
> 23rd October 19—

Dear Mr Stanley,

I will shortly be going to Birmingham on business and I wonder if you would be so kind as to give me a letter of introduction to your friend in the engineering trade up there. I should be very grateful to you.

Yours sincerely,

Letter asking a friend for a letter of introduction (2)

> 19 Cranleigh Gardens,
> Brighton.
>
> 23rd October 19—

Dear Paul,

As you may know, I have always wanted to work in book publishing. I have worked in a public library for three years, and previously on a local newspaper for a year.

I should be very grateful if you would give me a letter of introduction to the Editorial Director of Palmer's, who is, I believe, a great friend of yours, so that I could ask his advice on the best way to get into publishing.

I hope you will not mind my approaching you in this way.

Yours sincerely,

Reply agreeing

7 Manor Road,
Langley Moor.

27th October 19—

Dear Bill,

It was a very pleasant surprise to hear from you after all this time and to hear your news. I enclose a letter of introduction to my friend Tom Carter of Palmer's and hope that he may be able to find an opening for you in his publishing house or at least meet you for a chat.

Do let me know how you get on.

Yours sincerely,

Reply, less favourable

7 Manor Road,
Langley Moor.

27th October 19—

Dear Bill,

I was glad to hear from you again and to hear what you have been doing. Although I don't know Tom Carter particularly well, I will certainly mention you if I happen to run into him.

Yours sincerely,

Reply, refusing

7 Manor Road,
Langley Moor.

27th October 19—

Dear Bill,

Unfortunately I don't see Tom Carter of Palmer's very often
these days and I am afraid I will not have the chance of
mentioning your name to him. I am sorry I cannot help you
and hope a suitable post will turn up very soon.

Yours sincerely,

Letter of introduction (1)

7 Barlow House,
Upper Street,
London
SE26 8FG.

27th October 19—

Dear Mr Carter,

The bearer of this letter, Mr Frederick Jones, is a young
friend of mine, also in the engineering trade, who is visiting
your city on business.

Anything you can do to help him will be a kindness much
appreciated by him and, I need hardly say, by me.

Yours sincerely,

Letter of introduction (2)

40 Balcombe Crescent,
Lewisham.

2nd November 19—

Dear Mr Andrews,

A great friend of mine, Mr Nicholas Barlow, will be
spending Christmas and the New Year in Toronto. I know
you will get on well with him and perhaps make his stay in
your city at holiday time less lonely. He will be staying at the
Rapids Hotel from the end of this month and I do hope you
will have the time to get in touch with him.

Yours sincerely,

Thanks for letter of introduction

19 Cranleigh Gardens,
Brighton.

2nd November 19—

Dear Mr Stanley,

Thank you once again for the letter of introduction you
kindly gave me. Mr Carter gave me a most warm welcome as
well as a great deal of very valuable advice. He also put me
in touch with a number of important business contacts.

I am very grateful to you.

Yours sincerely,

Letter of thanks for kindness to a friend

7 Barlow House,
Upper Street,
London
SE26 8FG

5th November 19—

Dear Mr Carter,

I have to thank you very sincerely for your kind reception of
Frederick Jones. He tells me his trip has been both pleasant
and very successful, principally due to your help. I
appreciate it very much.

Yours sincerely,

Letter asking a friend for a loan

6 Lammas Lane,
London
SW18 6JV.

17th May 19—

Dear Malcolm,

I have not written to you without having given this matter
a great deal of thought. As you know my illness last year
meant that my financial affairs were thrown into disarray.
Unfortunately I have not yet got back to normal and I am
being pressed for payment of my debts by two long-standing
creditors.

In the circumstances, I wonder if you could possibly lend me
£X to tide me over the next couple of months. As you know
I am not the sort of person who normally borrows money

from friends but I just don't know what to do. I would be so very grateful if you could help me.

I hope this letter will not offend you in any way and if you cannot lend me the money I shall quite understand.

Yours sincerely,

Letter granting a loan

5 Harpenden Street,
London
SW4S 7BD.

21st May 19—

Dear Ann,

I was so sorry to hear of your financial plight and will of course be very happy to help you out. I therefore enclose a a cheque for £X. I certainly won't need this money before the autumn, so don't hurry to pay me back before you can afford it.

Yours sincerely,

Letter refusing a loan (1)

5 Harpenden Street,
London
SW4S 7BD.

21st May 19—

Dear Ann,

I was very distressed to receive your letter. All the more
since I cannot help you, my commitments being almost as
pressing as yours.

Why not have a chat with your bank manager about
your problems? He's the best person to give you advice and
I'm sure he'll find a way to help you. I do hope that everything
works out for you.

Every good wish.

Yours sincerely,

Letter refusing a loan (2)

5 Harpenden Street,
London
SW4S 7BD.

21st May 19—

Dear Ann,

I am very sorry but I am unable to help you. Although
I would be very glad to lend you the money, in the normal
course of events, I have rather a lot of expenses to meet at the
moment and a loan is out of the question. I sincerely hope
that things will soon take a turn for the better with you.

Yours ever,

152

Letter refusing a loan but offering a gift

5 Harpenden Street,
London
SW4S 7BD.

21st May 19—

Dean Ann,

I am so sorry to hear of your financial troubles. Although I have made a firm rule never to lend money to friends – it always seems to lead to trouble – I am enclosing a cheque for £X which I hope you will accept as a gift. I am sorry I cannot spare the full amount you need and hope your bank manager will be able to help you.

I do hope everything sorts itself out satisfactorily.

Yours sincerely,

Letter demanding repayment of a loan (1)

5 Harpenden Street,
London
SW4S 7BD.

7th December 19—

Dear Ann,

You'll remember that in May last year I lent you £X. At
that time I said I would not need the money until the autumn.
It is now nearly Christmas and I'm afraid I must ask you
to repay the loan as I badly need the money.

Yours sincerely,

Letter demanding payment of a loan (2)

5 Harpenden Street,
London
SW4 7BD.

17th December 19—

Dear Ann,

I must call your attention once again to the £X which you
borrowed from me several months ago. No doubt the matter
has escaped your attention and I hope you will be able to let
me have a cheque straight away.

Yours sincerely,

Letter demanding repayment of a loan and threatening to take legal action

5 Harpenden Street,
London
SW4S 7BD.

8th January 19—

Dear Ann,

I have already asked you several times about the money you owe me. I am sorry that I cannot wait any longer for it and if I do not receive a cheque from you by the end of the week I shall be forced to put the matter in the hands of my solicitors. I very much regret doing this, especially as I have always regarded you as a good friend, but I am rather hard up myself at the moment and unless you let me have the money I do not see what else I can do.

Yours sincerely,

A letter asking a solicitor to pursue a debt can be found on page 94.

Letter to a friend, asking him to act as Executor

7 Fairly Road,
Lymington,
Hampshire.

14 September 19—

Dear Ian,

I have decided at long last to make a will and would be delighted if you would agree to be one of my executors. My solicitor, Richard Cottenham, who will be drawing up the will is to be the other one.

If you feel that you cannot take on this responsibility, please do not be worried about telling me as I am sure I could find someone else, reluctant though I would be to do this.

Best wishes,

Letter to a friend asking him to act as Trustee

> The Yews,
> Boxmoor Road,
> Thames Ditton,
> Surrey.
>
> 9th August 19—

Dear Bob,

I am in the process of making my will and wonder whether you would be so kind as to allow me to appoint you an executor and also a Trustee in connection with the arrangements I am making for the children.

Your co-trustee would be Mr Simon Stephens, an old friend of mine and a solicitor of the highest integrity. In the event of the necessity arising you could call freely upon his expert advice.

I am asking you this favour principally because of our long friendship but also because you are a good deal younger than I am. If you feel able to accept these duties I would be very grateful to you and would certainly feel entirely happy about the future of the children.

Yours sincerely,

Classified advertisements

Although advertising in general is outside the scope of this book, many people may wish from time to time to sell an item through a newspaper advertisement.

An advertisement has a very special function; it must make an immediate impact on the casual reader and force him to read it more carefully, and to act upon it.

Advertising space is often expensive, and you should aim to put your message across in the least number of words possible. It is often a good idea to use abbreviations where they will be clearly understood.

Choose your advertising medium carefully by asking yourself 'do the people who want to buy this article read this journal?' Your local paper would be a good place to advertise your house for sale but if you are hoping to let your house for the summer you would have to advertise in a newspaper circulating outside your area.

Advertising a fund-raising event

Sat. October 1, 2 p.m. Jumble Sale St Mark's Church Admission Xp.

Art Exhibition by local artists at the parish hall on Friday 9th June from 2 p.m. to 5 p.m. Paintings can be purchased. Admission Xp. In aid of the children's home.

Advertising a club or society to attract new members

Woodbridge Angling Society. Membership open for adults. Monthly coach outing. Telephone:

Interested in gardening? Join the Grangewell Horticultural Society. Telephone: for details.

Advertising holiday accommodation

Holiday Cottage, Yorkshire Dales. Sleeps 6. C.H. Fully
Equipped. Available June onwards. Tel:

Windermere. Modern flat. Quiet location. Slps 4. £X week.
Tel:

Advertising a house or flat for sale

3-bedroomed semi-det. Wimbledon. Spacious kitchen.
Manageable garden. Garage. Freehold £X o.n.o. Tel:

PURLEY. Near station. 6-year-old detached house.
4 bedrooms. Double garage. C.H. and double glazing. £X.
Phone:

BRIGHTON. Self-contained ground-floor flat. 2 beds.
Lease 90 yrs. £X. Tel:

Advertising items for sale

6 oak dining chairs, plus carver. Seats and backs padded with
black leather and studded. £X. Tel:

As new Ranch Mink coat, size 12. £X. Tel:

Pram £X. Carrycot £X. Bath and stand £X. High chair £X.
Tel:

Ford (model) (year) excellent condition £X. Tel:

Advertising for domestic help

A capable help required for housework in large family house,
near station. Tuesdays and Fridays 10 a.m. to 1 p.m.
References required. Tel:

Gardener required once a week £X per hour. Tel:

Advertising a service

Home typist
Hard-working home typist offers fast efficient service. Will
collect and deliver. Tel:

Situations Wanted

Young, hardworking English Honours Graduate, keen to
make career in bookselling. Please write to E. Kray,
86 Queens Road, Guildford.

Tradesman commencing business

James Clayton will be opening a spacious Do-it-Yourself
supply stores at 3 Billet Road on Friday 5th June. The most
up-to-date and highest quality merchandise will be offered
at discount prices. The shop will carry vast stocks of sawn
and planed timber, plywood, plastic laminates, paints and
wallpapers and all the tools for the D-I-Y enthusiast.

Tradesman soliciting custom

Whitney's School of Motoring. Door to door service. Dual
control cars. Tel: